FROM THE ALLEGHENIES TO THE HEBRIDES

An Autobiography

Margaret Fay Shaw

BIRLINN

This edition first published in 2008 by
Birlinn Limited
West Newington House
10 Newington Road
Edinburgh
EH9 1QS

www.birlinn.co.uk

First published in 1993 by
Canongate Books Ltd, Edinburgh

ISBN13: 978 1 84158 770 7
ISBN10: 1 84158 770 2

British Library Cataloguing-in-Publication Data
A catalogue record for this book is available from the British Library

Printed and bound by CPI Cox & Wyman, Reading, RG1 8EX

Contents

Acknowledgements

Writing this book and putting it together has required endless help from Ann Evans Berthoff. I am also indebted to Robin Humes for typing the manuscript, and to Hugh Cheape for checking the proofs with such diligence. I am grateful to the Scottish Arts Council and to the many friends whose encouragement made this book's publication possible. Finally I want to thank Kathleen Raine for giving me permission to use two of her poems in my book.

.

Foreword

Some years ago I was at a dinner party in New York. I left with another guest well after midnight to find a taxi. It was not a yellow cab but obviously one that belonged to the driver. It had no light inside. A very large man drove with his left hand while his right arm was extended along the seat. From Central Park West we crossed to Fifth Avenue and 60th Street where we left my companion at her club. Then we started to Park Avenue and to my destination at the far end on the edge of Harlem. He drove at a crawl and asked me where we two ladies came from as he liked our accents. I said that the lady came from London and I came from Pennsylvania but lived in Scotland. And where did he come from? 'A little town in Arkansas you never heard of – but what took you to Scotland?' We continued to travel at a snail's pace.

I found myself telling him my life history and when I told him of the Island of Canna, that it was a farm, he asked me questions that were a pleasure to answer. The kind of sheep, the quality of their wool, the cattle, what I meant by 'hill cattle' and 'Highland cattle', the crops, the weather.

'Lady,' he said, 'you should write a book. It's the kind of book I like to read and make it two generations.' And when we reached my door he thanked me for giving him my story and said, 'Lady, you write that book and remember it was a New York taxi driver that inspired you to do it.'

Introduction

So much of Margaret Fay Shaw's life was summed up in aphorisms and metaphors, either her own or others as she recounted them, when in later life she described herself for example as 'a bird blown off course'. We might imagine that this stood for the highly unusual outcome of a young American settling in the Scottish Hebrides in the 1920s, but Margaret's life can be perceived more broadly as a flight from constraints and conventionality. As her account unfolds, we sense a flight from social and family constraints away like a migrating bird to new experiences of place and people in regions then unimaginable to her compatriots of the Alleghenies. Though loyal to her adopted country, she remained robustly independent throughout her long life and deprecated in lively terms the tribal behaviour and complacency of cosmopolitan Scots. Evident in the structure of this autobiographical account, her life was measured out in a series of dramatic personal episodes themed by strength of character and indomitable will and spirit sustaining her in a course largely going against the flow. When facing up to the forces of constraint and convention, she would frequently say, reminding us of her love for the land of her birth and pride of ancestry: 'I'm made of Pittsburgh steel!'

Her independence or 'flight' was never sentimental or escapist as her own achievements demonstrate. What might seem unremarkable interests in an educated twentieth-century individual, in music, in reading and writing, in photography, in the appreciation of the tangible and intangible, take on the quality of the extraordinary in Margaret's life of changing and varied fortunes. In terms of the times, she engaged with people in a highly unconventional but uniquely personal way, disregarding entirely social mores, and became the distinguished collector and editor of

Scottish Gaelic song and traditional material, as well as photographer and recorder of a Hebridean way of life.

Born at the old family home of Glenshaw, near Pittsburgh in Pennsylvania, on 9 November 1903, she was the fifth and youngest of the children of a civil engineer of Scottish descent, Henry Clay Shaw, and Fanny Maria Patchin of a New England family. In childhood she thrived on the personal and spontaneous but rebelled against the formalities of upbringing and education. In 1921 she was sent to school in Scotland for a year following the death of her parents. She heard the song collector and 'Celtic-Romantic' doyenne, Marjory Kennedy Fraser, singing her 'Songs of the Hebrides' at St Bride's School, Helensburgh, and was inspired to learn about Hebridean music and song. She describes how these were impressive as 'art songs' but that qualitatively different music as well as the Gaelic language lay behind them. These she pursued after a classical training studying piano in New York, London and Paris. Piquantly described travels led to Uist and a transcendental attraction that changed her life.

Margaret went to stay in South Uist in 1928 and the next six years were spent in the house of Peggy and Mary MacRae in Glendale, South Lochboisdale. The communities of Loch Boisdale lay at the centre of Margaret's affections and supplied a deeply sincere and recurring refrain which fascinated friends and scholars over the years. The people of South Uist were her big family. Here she learnt Gaelic and took down songs, stories and traditional material from the MacRae sisters and from their neighbours in the Uist crofting townships. This work was done with great care and without the aid of any recording equipment. It required a thorough knowledge of the language and a musical skill and agility to transcribe a complex of modes and scales. In Gaelic song, the words and music are highly integrated and the phonetic structure of the language among the most complicated in the world. She describes how she had to forget the major and minor scales of the classically trained pianist and had to listen and learn. She based her editorial technique on a book of folksongs which she had bought in

Dublin in 1927, following a chance-meeting with Mrs Costelloe of Tuam, a senator from County Mayo. The latter, as Eibhlín Bean Mhic Choistealbha, had published the collection *Amhráin Mhuighe Seóla* with the Talbot Press in 1923 and included full texts, provenance, sources and proper *apparatus criticus*.

During this time Margaret also made films and took photographs of life in the Islands and further afield and these have been used in journals, books and broadcasting over the years. The odyssey outlined in the chapters that follow is matched by a graphic storehouse illustrating trips to Galway and the Aran Islands, Barra, Mingulay and St Kilda, which she visited in May 1930 on the eve of evacuation. With the passage of time, the archive which Margaret Fay Shaw built up has emerged as a unique and precious view of the Hebrides; this was not the fancy of the passing tourist but the life's work of one who had dedicated her career to the study of disappearing ways of life in the British Isles and of one who took the trouble to learn the language and to live within and understand the culture which she has subsequently written on with such cogency and conviction. For her photography and a lifetime's achievement, the Royal Scottish Geographical Society awarded Margaret Honorary Fellowship in November 2004.

Margaret Fay Shaw's sojourn and research work in Uist between 1929 and 1935 bore fruit principally in her *Folksongs and Folklore of South Uist,* published in 1955 and later republished by Oxford University Press (1977), Aberdeen University Press (1986) and in a high quality paperback edition by Birlinn Limited (1999). This was a pioneering view of what might now be described as the 'cultural environment', giving extraordinarily important insights into island life in the twentieth century and increasing our understanding of it in so many ways. A selection of songs forms the core of the book and reflects the enriching role of music in a way of life; they include songs in praise of home and Uist, love-song, lullabies, laments and songs of exile, 'mouth music' or *puirt-a-beul* as songs for dancing and entertainment, milking songs, spinning songs, waulking songs or *orain luadhaidh*, clapping songs and 'quern songs'. Beyond the songs and musical scores, she included stories and anecdotes, prayers, proverbs, cures (for folk and animals in equal measure), charms and recipes. Margaret's eye and sense of detail enhance and lend colour to the anecdotes of people and place in this book. The same innate skill garnered the cultural wealth of a single small community, as testimony to one of the richest tradition-bearing societies of Europe. Her *Folksongs and Folklore* received important plaudits from overseas scholars. Recognition of the significance of her work for example came from Scandinavia, where scholars had made the languages and culture of the Hebrides and Northern Isles very much their business. Professor Magne Oftedal, in reviewing *Folksongs* in the journal *Lochlann*, commented that '. . . the collection as a whole carries the imprint of great accuracy, reliability, and faithfulness to the sources . . .'.

Similar praise from Nordic and Irish scholars had accrued to Margaret's husband, the folklorist John Lorne Campbell, whom she had met in Lochboisdale in 1934. They married in 1935 and settled first in Barra and then in the island of Canna, which Dr Campbell bought in 1938. Canna remained their home thereafter and was gifted to the National Trust for Scotland in 1981. Setting up home in Canna, sustaining an island way of life through wartime conditions and developing a Hebridean farming enterprise form the closing chapters of Margaret's book. Chiming with her keen affection for the patriarchs of the Celtic Church, Margaret's story concludes on a June day in 1963 with a service in Canna to celebrate the 1,400th anniversary of St Columba's coming to Scotland. Canna, with its dedication to Colum Cille, was part of the founding Saint's domain and a sanctuary frequented by him.

This commemoration, glowingly described, concludes Margaret's book, but those who knew her would protest that the story never ended there. She lived on in Canna for over forty years, surviving John Lorne's Campbell's death in 1996 until her own on 11 December 2004.

Music so often greeted the visitor in Canna House and no one who was present will forget Margaret taking to the piano at her hundredth birthday party in Canna and moving with ease between Strauss waltzes and Uist songs first heard by her in the 1920s. She rejoiced in the company of friends and the atmosphere of *cèilidh* which had been sustained unabatingly. This was captured in Neil Fraser's warm hundredth-birthday tribute, 'Among Friends', broadcast at the time by the BBC.

Margaret was a charming hostess and the presiding genius of an old-world elegance and hospitality which could be said to have evoked the tacksmen's houses of the old Hebrides as described by Samuel Johnson and James Boswell in 1773. Visitors were attentively cared for with catering from a well-tended Canna House garden and in the ambience of a subtle blend of Georgian, Colonial and Art Nouveau plenishing and décor. Acceptance of Canna House's kindness meant instant familiarity with the attendant tribe of cats, a natural pantheon of household gods with whom Margaret was in constant communication.

'I don't even have a Sunday school certificate', was Margaret's self-deprecatory comment on her own education, but, for her *Folksongs and Folklore of South Uist* and other research papers as well as for her extensive photographic work, she was given Honorary Degrees by St Francis Xavier University, Nova Scotia, The National University of Ireland in Dublin, and Aberdeen and Edinburgh Universities. Together with the late John Lorne Campbell's libraries, archives and sound recording collections, Margaret created an extraordinary integrity for and contribution to Scottish and Gaelic studies worldwide.

Hugh Cheape
Sabhal Mòr Ostaig
Colaiste Ghàidhlig na h-Alba
St Patrick's Day 2008

CHAPTER ONE

Glenshaw, Sewickley,
Bryn Mawr, Helensburgh

IT WAS IN 1782 when my great-great-grandfather, John Shaw, arrived in Philadelphia from Scotland with his four sons. He was given a large grant of land in the west of the state to be divided among the sons. The one who was my great-grandfather, Thomas Wilson Shaw, chose the low-lying valley of Pine Creek and there, in 1823, built his house of bricks fired on the place – the walls four bricks thick – and a small factory where he made sickles, hoes, and ploughs for the settlers who were opening the new land. Two young surveyors arrived from Scotland and stayed with him. A survey map of the whole property was needed and there was to be a post office, so a name for the place had to be found and one of the surveyors named Munro suggested 'Glenshaw'. In time, Thomas Wilson Shaw prospered. He built a church in a field near his house and set aside a piece of ground for his grandson, my father, to build a house. There I was born, the youngest of five daughters.

Glenshaw is a narrow wooded valley with a stream we called 'The Crick' and a road made of planks. The two hillsides were thick with trees, mountain laurel and sassafras, with trillium and jack-in-the-pulpits in spring. The shallow creek with the flat rocks was where we played, catching crayfish and shivering at the sight of the occasional water-snake. The wide lawn stretched from our house on past the old house with its giant elms and maple trees, the apple trees, and then the barn, big and mysterious with the lovely smell of horses and leather. Up above was the hayloft where we would climb onto a beam at some peril and jump off into the mountain of hay.

By the barn grew an apple tree which bore what we called the July apples for they were the first to ripen. We children would gather the first that fell and hide them in the hay-mow to ripen. They were small, yellow with red stripes, and I have never tasted their like – the best ever. There were other apple trees, Northern Spy was one, and they were for cooking or eating, and some for making apple butter. A huge iron cauldron was placed on a wood fire outside, under the sycamore tree, and filled with sour apples flavoured with cinnamon, spice, and sugar. The great aunts, Maria the cook, and anyone tall enough would take turns stirring with a long-handled paddle with several holes in it. Shaped like a hoe, it was pushed back and forth for hours until the mixture was a dark ruddy brown. Then it was put in Mason jars. I have never found the recipe in any cookery book. It may have been made only by country people who could have an outside fire and the large pot and paddle – a recipe handed down.

The family legend is that Mrs Heinz first made her ketchup in a copper cauldron borrowed from the Glenshaw kitchen. It is now in the museum of the Western Pennsylvania Historical Society.

Behind the barn there was a narrow path above the hayfield made of two narrow planks with a wooden railing. It was overhung with elder bushes, first laden with white blossom and then the masses of deep purple berries. The path ended at a little wicket gate that I was forbidden to pass, for there was the high bank and the tunnel through the hill – the Baltimore and Ohio Railroad. The trains came roaring up the valley, blowing their whistles and ringing their bells, rushing like thunder into the tunnel. A great cloud of black smoke would come out after they passed. How I longed to see what was on the other side of the tunnel! For me it was through the tunnel that the great wide world lay. I watched the long line of freight cars with their steady slow speed and the little house at the end that had

a chimney called a caboose. I heard that that was the way to travel:
hop a freight and lie flat on the top. Then the fast trains with the
sleeping cars bound for Chicago came streaking past and away
through the tunnel. Billy White was the engineer, and his mother
lived in Glenshaw.

My great-grandfather lived to be ninety-six. He told my father how
as a little boy *his* father had lifted him up on his shoulders to see
General Washington pass by on a white horse, when he came to
Pittsburgh. My grandfather, Thomas Wilson Shaw, was a surgeon
at Gettysburg and a doctor for the immigrants in the slums of
Pittsburgh who had come to work in the mills. He was a man
who never sent out his bills and was greatly loved. He served
as an interne and then stayed as a doctor at Mercy Hospital, the
first Catholic hospital in Pittsburgh, where the nurses were nuns.
Thomas Wilson Shaw was a Presbyterian but the nuns adored
him. When my sister Kay first went as a pathologist to work with
Dr Willetts in the 1930s, an elderly nun came in with a young nun
who needed attention, saw my sister's name on the door and said,
'Are you by any chance a relation of a Doctor Thomas Shaw?'
They were still making up his purge pills, known as 'Dr Shaw's
Little Black Devils'.

My father, Henry Shaw, was the eldest son and his father's pride.
He was a civil engineer, a graduate of Rensselaer, already a famous
college of engineering. He had wanted to be an artist and had shown
some talent in portrait painting, but my grandfather regarded artists
as Bohemians in velvet jackets and flowing ties, supported by their
parents. My father bought pictures to enjoy and his greatest delight
was seeing the International Exhibition of paintings that came to the
Carnegie Museum once a year. It was famous and brought visitors
from Europe as well as from the United States. He longed to visit
London and when he was recovering from pneumonia and in need
of a change from Pittsburgh's foul air, he and my mother sailed in
February to London, the worst of climates. People in the hotel were

shocked that he wouldn't stand in the cold to see King Edward pass by but *had* gone through snow to hear Campbell Bannerman, the famous leader of the Liberals, speak in Parliament. And he returned with a fine collection of etchings which he greatly prized. One was of Dr Samuel Johnson's house in Gough Square. The Doctor was his idol.

John Shaw and his sons had continued their trade as iron founders. It was said that John iron-cast the first cannon west of the Alleghenies. The small factory started by his son, the first Thomas Wilson, produced a sickle which must have been to his own design, for there isn't its like anywhere in the United States. His grandson, my father, continued the family tradition: he was the head of the Garrison Foundry, a steel mill in Pittsburgh on the south side of the Monongahela River. He knew every man in the mill – many were Czechs, and the warmth and good feeling among them was my father's pride. The mill made steel rollers used in the manufacture of, among other things, Peters Chocolate silver paper wrappers and Kellogg's Corn Flakes. When I was seven, my father took me to see the fiery molten steel being poured into the sand moulds – a fearsome sight – and to meet the mules which pulled the heavy loads. They were black and enormous, but they bent their heads to allow me to stroke their soft white, velvety noses.

My father was extremely well read. Every Christmas, his five daughters would give him a novel of George Eliot in the Nelson green leather edition. He and my mother gave each other books and marked for one another passages they'd enjoyed. They were both very active in the Pittsburgh Civic Club, trying to improve housing for the immigrants who'd come to work in the mills. He voted for Wilson because he liked the man; he couldn't abide Teddy Roosevelt – forget just why, but I'm sure he'd have opposed anyone who was so pugnacious. I remember his reaction to an incident at school. We once had a substitute named Mrs Good, who looked like an American Indian, with black hair and eyes and a long dark face. She laboured to teach us the parsing and constructing of sentences, but her temper was violent. One day she said, 'Charles Hanlin, if you don't shut your mouth, you'll see your length on the floor!' I thought it was a wonderful sentence, but when I told my father at the dining table that evening, he was not only horrified at Mrs Good's language but that I should repeat it.

My mother was a New England Yankee from Vermont, where breeding and mental ability were what mattered. Her maternal ancestor, Joseph Patchin, came from England as a bonded servant to Connecticut in 1640. In the following hundred years, the Patchins married into well-known New England families and eventually settled in Old Bennington. I think she found the wealth, without the distinguished minds, of the Pittsburghers difficult to take. But she had in my father a like mind in taste and in books.

My two great-aunts and great-uncle lived in the house built by their father in the 1820s. They spent their summer afternoons in their splendid wicker chairs on the porch with its four white pillars. They had pockets in these chairs to hold their books and the big palm-leaf fans that they used slowly and elegantly. Once, on a hot afternoon, the two aunts were having a call from the preacher. Their conversation was interrupted by the simple-minded son of a neighbour who appeared with a bucket. 'Mum wants to know if she can have some of your well water. Our spring's warm as piss.' 'Take it, take it,' said Aunt Mat, rocking furiously.

My great-aunts were a contrast. Aunt Ellen was small and stout with a sharp tongue and a keen wit, while Aunt Martha was tall and large. Looking up beside her, it seemed a mile to her belt with the silver buckle. Her loving kindness was a warm cloud around her great frame.

The old house – the Big House, as we called it – was always cool on the hottest day. The room known as the front parlour was only opened for special callers and tea parties in summer. It was a light and pretty room with a white marble mantelpiece and the portraits of the great-grandparents. In winter it was piercing cold; one time it was said to be below zero. But the living room and dining room were warm and welcoming.

If there was illness or company in our house we were sent to stay in the Big House and this was an adventure. The beds were enormous and one sank deep in the feather mattress with a mass of bedclothes on top. A hot brick wrapped in flannel warmed the frigid feet. The first sound in the morning was the coffee mill which Maria held between her knees to grind. Then the little drawer in it would be opened and a heaped tablespoon to each cup of cold water put in the big coffee pot to boil, then an eggshell to clear it. Breakfast was always with Maria, in the kitchen: buckwheat cakes with maple syrup, wheaten cakes with hot molasses and butter, corn meal mush or porridge. We would linger on until told by Maria, 'Lick up your molasses and then you're done!'

The Nash family figures in my earliest memories of Glenshaw. Maria was the mother of Louie, the gardener and houseman, his wife Birdie was our cook and their little boy Harry, who was near the age of my sister Biddy, was our companion. Louie had interesting knowledge of his father who had been a slave on a plantation in Virginia, coming originally from Nigeria. Biddy and Harry started their first days at school together. I remember my mother entrusting Harry to pull the little wagon on which was a large glass bowl of goldfish for their class to admire.

A neighbour farmer, Mr Glasgow, always brought pork sausage when he killed a pig in winter weather. And how cold the winter! The creek was frozen hard and there was skating on the mill pond. The snow lay deep and one knew from the special squeak of the wagon wheels that it was below zero. We children enjoyed sleigh rides with the many small bells on the horses ringing; straw filled the sleigh to keep us warm, and we huddled together with the thought of hot chocolate and cake at the end of the ride. It would be so cold that we put bananas on the window-sill when we went to bed, and in the morning they were frozen as hard as stone and we chipped off pieces. So delicious! Then a thaw would come and the ice on The Crick would crack like the sound of a gun. One time it formed a great gorge a long way up the valley. My father, hurrying home from the train, warned us that the gorge was about to break and would bring a flood. We sat by the fire listening. Soon we heard the sound of water in the dark. It filled the cellar and my father, with his trousers rolled up his thin white legs, went to rescue the laundry which was afloat in the baskets. Then the water was above his knees and he came up the cellar stairs, worried about the Big House for, the year that I was born, it had come in several inches deep and the best carpet in the front parlour was frozen to the floor. We peered out the window in the blackness and could see the shine of lighted windows on the water and great white lumps of ice were banging against the house and floating away in the dark.

The next morning found us marooned. Enormous great cakes of ice, like plinths of giant statues, were everywhere. The whole valley was a frozen lake. My sisters put on their skates and sailed off to the Big House to find that all was well, then on across the lawn and through the meadow. What gaiety this catastrophe brought! My father managed to scramble from the back door to the hillside and found his way to the village and came back laden mostly with baked beans. There was no gas so we dined from a chafing dish, which was much more fun. There were no trains and no post, no school for my sisters for several days. Everyone was skating. So many Shaws – uncles, aunts, countless cousins, and four older sisters. I, being the youngest, was spoilt one hour and bullied the next. I was bundled up to watch the skating and just as a very pretty cousin leant down to give me a kiss, a young man put his dirty hand between her lips and my cheek.

Even in summer, the shallow creek where we loved to play and whose gentle song we could hear as we lay in bed could become a raging torrent sweeping across the lawn, surrounding the houses, washing away the planks that made the road, and the bridges, as it swept on to the Allegheny River. Then it would quietly return to its proper place and the yellow water would clear. We would wade in the pools that were left in the garden and catch the tiny minnows in the grass. Once, the water filled the cellar and washed out the mushroom beds of manure from the dark recesses. But there was little destruction compared to what happened in a village called The Flats further down the valley. Mrs Mauser was carried away while seated in her outdoor privy, which fortunately lodged between two trees. She was gallantly rescued, but I was horrified thinking of her embarrassment. I was told that that would not trouble Mrs Mauser. It was afterwards known as 'Mrs Mauser's gondola'.

Automobiles were appearing and our more well-to-do relations would come from their fine houses to call on their country kin in large Pierce Arrow limousines with liveried chauffeurs. The seats were of fine leather, but in summer they were covered in white linen. We were sometimes taken to visit these relatives and I enjoyed their elegance but was so shy that I could scarcely speak when spoken to and had a painful time swallowing at table. 'Don't you like your orange juice?' Of course I loved it but felt I made such a noise swallowing that I was ashamed to drink it.

One year my father's young widowed sister with her little boy and various uncles took our house for the summer while we lived in the Big House, the great-aunts having gone to California. The little boy brought his pony with a governess cart, a thing we had never seen before. Our world had only buggies and surreys and what we called a 'trap'. How I longed to ride in that two-wheeled contraption that looked like a giant laundry-basket, but my mother forbade me to ask. I stood in the drive watching them jump in. I could bear it no longer, and I said, 'Here's me!' The kind uncle lifted me up. I hadn't asked and I now think I was extraordinarily astute for a child of four.

On rare occasions I was taken to Pittsburgh – 'town' as we called it. My sister Martha took my nearest sister Biddy and myself to the Nixon Theatre to see 'The Bluebird' by Maeterlinck. We were so excited, dressed in our beaver hats and Peter Thomson coats, navy blue with brass buttons and an eagle on the sleeves. First the train ride and then the sight of this wonderful theatre in red plush, white and gold! I was spellbound until Tyltyl, the black cat, cried at the door to be let in. Such a passion for cats I have that I was desperate, seeing one in such a state. I cried out, 'Let him in, let him in!' Poor Martha was so embarrassed and I was soon in tears and disgrace.

Another time Martha took me to see Beerbohm Tree as Wolsey in Henry VIII. I can see him today in his long scarlet robes with his arms raised, clutching a great iron gate and crying, 'If I had served my God!' Another scene I will never forget was the dance with Anne Boleyn in a beautiful voluminous pink dress, stepping so gracefully to lovely tunes. Later I tried to play them and many years after found they had been composed by Edward German. This monumental thrill would have been in 1912.

There was, too, a memorable visit to the Carnegie Museum. It involved not only the train to town, but a trolley-car ride to this enormous grey stone building. Such a hush was inside! My sister Martha's one reason for taking me was to see what she called the 'dipple-a-dockus'. The complete bones of this reptile had recently been put together, and it was the biggest ever found. I was appalled at the sight, though I was told it would wear a thick grey hide and only eat vegetables. I saw it again in a dream when I looked from my bedroom window to see that The Crick had been in flood and had subsided to leave the valley a sea of yellow mud. Half-buried in the mud was a railway engine and very near at hand stood the dipple-a-dockus. It looked amiable but not pleasant.

My enthusiasm for cats was shared with my father but not my mother. They were given Old Testament names and my special favourite was Tiglath-Pilezar. My great-aunt Ellen was fond of cats and explained to me that the reason her toms grew to such an extraordinary size was because she always heated their milk in a tin cup on the stove. I was told of a terrible calamity when my sister Martha dropped a kitten in the milk churn. But since it was my great-aunt Martha churning, all was forgiven. Dogs were not allowed because there had been a case of rabies and my father was nervous, especially in the heat of summer. Yet he was fond of dogs and talked of a splendid one he loved called Rip who was also a favourite of Aunt Ellen's. Rip was buried under the trees at the edge of the creek in a lovely spot. Aunt Ellen said to my father, 'You can bury me here, and put up a stone for both of us – "Here lies Aunt Ellen, doggone her, let her Rip".' Aunt Ellen, with her smart black bonnet tied under the chin with broad ribbons, so small, neat and assured, a pillar of the church and the missionary society, had no illusions nor awe. My father went with her to attend the funeral of an elderly relative by marriage who had been a missionary in China. The family knew that he had been very hard on their gentle cousin, who had had a raft of children whose clothes came from missionary boxes and who died at an early age. But the minister extolled the virtues of this man, carrying the message of Christ to the heathen: 'He shall be found in the bosom of Abraham.' Aunt Ellen whispered, 'Harry, wouldn't he make a handsome breast pin!'

My sister Biddy and I loved to stay at the Big House. In the evenings, Great-Aunt Ellen would tell the exciting stories of the adventures of her relations. Her Aunt Baird lived in a log cabin on what was the Indian trail north to Erie. Once, a bear leaned over the half-door to remove a ham which hung from a hook in the ceiling. There were stories of the troubles which her forebears had during the French and Indian Wars of 1756–63. One young wife with her new baby was warned by her husband to climb the ladder to the loft as the Indians were coming. She was no sooner in the loft when an Indian came in demanding food, pinning her husband to the wall. Now she had been making soap and had the cauldron in the loft to cool. It was still hot when she poured it down on both husband and Indian. The Indian fled and the husband was able to shut and bar the door. Their neighbour, who kept his rifle above the door, was reaching for it when an arrow pierced his heart.

There was a half-breed Indian guide called Simon Gerties who served both sides. Aunt Ellen's great-grandmother knew him well and had been kind to him. He arrived at her cabin to tell her that the Indians were on the warpath and burning cabins: she must go at once to Fort Duquesne. Her several children were about to eat their meal, and when she insisted that they eat first, he yanked the cloth from the table, put the children in panniers on the ponies' backs, and so they started for the Fort. They arrived safely and shortly after a baby was born. Long afterwards, this daughter married a prosperous merchant in Pittsburgh named Dilworth. He had a portrait painted of his aged mother-in-law, which long hung in the dining-room of the house at Glenshaw.

In the fall, when the weather was turning really cold, a tiny, thin little woman would arrive at the Big House to spend the winter. She was known as Irish Katie, and what she did to assist the great-aunts for her lodging we never knew. She spent the summers wandering the country roads selling needles, pins, thread and such things from her large basket – what Aunt Ellen called 'canvassing'. Biddy and I were enthralled by her stories when she would join us by the evening dining-room fire. What a wonderful country was Ireland! There were leprechauns – she had seen them herself – little wee men that wore green caps. You had to be very nice to them or they would turn very nasty, but they were good to the poor. Then she told of a wicked man who rode in a carriage to collect rents from the poor, and how they had waited for him one dark night, hiding behind the gate of the grand house to grab the horses, drag him out and kill him. This story she told us with such delight and satisfaction. To that moment, all stories we had been told had happy endings; this one gave me a strange fear. With the first sign of spring, Irish Katie disappeared. I was told by Aunt Ellen that she was off on the road where she belonged. There was no keeping her in a civilised house. She would probably be found dead in a ditch.

My father tried to persuade me that most snakes were harmless and beautiful, making me stand beside him while he tickled a harmless black-snake with a long piece of straw so that it curled up and shot out its forked tongue. Black-snakes were the friend of man, and the water snakes in The Crick would do no harm unless we stood on them. But I knew there were copperheads about and they were poisonous enough to make one very ill if bitten. My friend Rosalia was playing in the grape arbour one hot Sunday afternoon and began to cry. Her aunt took off her sandal and sock to see the two marks of the fangs. She at once began to suck the wound, and the only car in the village was sent for to take her to town to hospital, where she stayed quite a while. From that time on, we were made to wear boots when playing in the long grass.

Aunt Ellen's tomcat brought in a snake and left it on the flagstones at the kitchen door. We all gathered to see it and were told by our young nursemaid that it wouldn't die until sundown. I showed the most fear, so she took it by the tail and chased me, whirling it around and then letting go. It struck me in the back. I ran so fast and tried to scream, but no sound came. After that I had dreadful nightmares. A snake was in the goldfish bowl, and I could see its white underside as it moved against the glass. My sister's long brown pigtail on the pillow in the night made me scream. I was a long time getting over this fear, until some years later I made myself pick one up by the tail. I found it dry and firm, not like what I had imagined. It cured me of my phobia.

There were wild animals in the wood. The most lovable were the raccoons. So fat and thick-coated with stubby ringed tails, and bright sweet faces. They were a pest, but my father had forbidden hunting of any kind. They would come down at night in a band to take the ears of corn off the stalks, never finishing one but they liked to taste many. They could remove lids from garbage pails and had a fondness for cake and sugar. We had a tame one that lived in a pen built around a tree. He had to have a pan of water, for everything given him he would take in his little hand-like paws and wash thoroughly, whether it was bread or a crayfish.

Weasels were the great menace. If they could get in the hen house they would murder every one, sucking the blood. One day a fine red fox carried off one of my father's precious Rhode Island Reds, but he was so delighted that such a rare animal should be in the vicinity, he ignored the crime. Possums would come to steal the eggs and one gorged himself and then fell asleep in a nest. I saw him there as I tiptoed in, such a lovely fur coat but a long and scaly tail. I was distressed because Louie took him away to be roasted for a party.

Louie was a wonderful friend, always patient with questions and showing me many exciting things. Once he took me through the snow to the Crick bank. The ice on either side didn't quite meet and the water ran swiftly between. There on the opposite side was a brown mink with her two striped kittens clinging to her back. She was busy fishing. I remember Louie's anger when the orange cat, Caesar, walked up the back steps which he had just finished painting green. My sister cried to him from the kitchen door, 'Poor Caesar, how shall I get the paint off?' Louie had an answer: 'You bring me a kettle of boiling water . . .!'

Being the youngest of five sisters, with three years between myself and my sister Biddy, I was left alone to find my pleasures. I can still hear the voice of Chick-a-biddy as I tried to follow her and her friends: 'Do we have to take her?' But I concluded that to tag along would be grim, and I had other interests. Music was a joy, even when it brought tears. My father gave my mother a phonograph that played wax cylinders, but they were distressed when, upon hearing 'My Darling Nellie Gray', I flung myself in my mother's lap and was hard to console. It was my first taste of woe. I much preferred listening as my cousin Charlie would sing 'Susan Brown' to his guitar, or 'Over the Banister Leans a Face', and my favourite, 'Beauty's Eyes'. All his songs were cheerful and full of love. Sad songs were a disaster.

But the great temptation was the piano. Caroline was the sister who first showed musical talent; she was given lessons by a German professor in Pittsburgh. *I* was not to touch the piano, for it was hers to practice and play. But when she was out of the house, I would touch the keys and find a tune. One day as I tried both hands, I suddenly found my tune and played 'All Through the Night'. Louie was polishing the stairs and showed his astonishment. The key I had hit upon had six sharps and remained so for all my tunes until I added five flats. I was limited to those two keys. To this day, I can't play the simplest thing in the key of G by ear, but I can be blind and play in six sharps. Now the piano is, after all, a modern instrument. Why is it that somebody born today plays in that key without any training at all? I don't understand it. This habit of playing by ear in those two keys from the age of six (and ever after) proved a great handicap when I started my music lessons at twelve.

My father was delighted, and from that time he took me to hear the very rare little concerts that came to Glenshaw. (Most of the music at Glenshaw came from the church choir, which sometimes had the accompaniment of a string quartet. I disliked contraltos and 'cellos which to me were dark brown and sad.) I remember the first time vividly: four men called the 'Bell Ringers from London' came to Glenshaw and arranged their innumerable bells on a long table in the church. Two men in evening dress gave us a taste of their art, playing with such agility and ease that the audience had the thrill of their lives. But the day above all others was when my father took me to Pittsburgh to hear Sousa's band play in a giant concert hall. 'Stars and Stripes Forever' and Liszt's 'Hungarian Rhapsody Number Two' stayed in my head until I found their titles long afterwards.

I did not go to school until I was seven. A young lady in the village started what was then unknown, a kindergarten, and I attended in the mornings to learn to put beads on a string and paint with exciting bright colours the daubs to take home to my mother. It was she who taught me to read. I sat on a low stool by her knee while she embroidered initials on white damask napkins, two tight rings holding the surface flat. I was far more interested in a big black dog called Rover than in her progress, but a tap of her thimble on the top of my head brought me to mind.

* * *

It was at Easter time that my mother died. I was seven years old. My sister Biddy and I had been taken to stay with a family friend away from our valley where this sorrow was to come. The friend took me on her knee to tell me my mother had gone to Heaven. In my misery and tears, I told my first lie. She asked me if I was using a handkerchief and I said 'yes'; but it was my doll's dress. This was on my conscience for years.

Why is it that grown women will talk together before a child of all the pity and worry they feel, as if the child were deaf and could not have any understanding? Then there was the embarrassment of returning to school, which was thought would be the cure for my grief. The stares and silence from the other children were too hard to bear. I ran off one afternoon, crossed the Crick and hid in the woods, where I found relief and interest in the flowers and in being alone. When I thought school would be out, I walked through the wood to the village where I would meet the other children to come home. It was too early. My way took me through the back-yard of an elderly cousin. She saw me and called me to come to her porch where she had milk and cookies waiting. She never asked me where or why, and she never told. I loved her forever.

My father decided that we would move over the hills to the village of Sewickley on the Ohio River, where he had sisters and brothers to comfort and advise him on bringing up his five daughters. He had pleasure in rebuilding a house there. But it was a contrast to the lovely woods, fields, and freedom of Glenshaw. No more Louie, Birdie, or little Harry, to my sorrow – and then Alice, whose loving arms knew what I missed. She wore her spotless white aprons so stiff with starch that I cut my lip on the hem when I flung myself into her lap. I still have the scar.

I remember sitting on the steps of the house at Glenshaw looking down the valley towards the place where it makes a sharp bend, and there on the hillside was a sheer rock that used to catch the red glow of the sunset. I had watched for that glow so many times.

Long afterwards I found in a poem of Emily Dickinson's lines that bring back that desolate day:

> There's a certain slant of light
> On winter afternoons,
> That oppresses, like the weight
> Of cathedral tunes.
>
> . . . .
>
> When it comes the landscape listens,
> Shadows hold their breath;
> When it goes, 'tis like the distance
> On the look of death.

Sewickley is on the bank of the Ohio River, some twenty miles over the hills from Glenshaw. People used to refer to it as a village, but it was much more like a small town, with two banks, many shops, a police station with two cells, and a fire-engine house. Along the tree-lined streets were the fine houses of the well-to-do, while up the hill were the splendid estates of the very wealthy. It was and still is the elite suburb of Pittsburgh.

My sister Martha, who was next to eldest, had returned from boarding school to take the responsibility of being mother to me and of the house, which at the age of eighteen was a heavy load. It would have been easier to go on living in Glenshaw, where we belonged, and where we had no overseers. In Sewickley we were surrounded by aunts; Martha was determined that my sister Biddy and I should appear before them as models of neatness and good behaviour.

Biddy was all that could be desired in both accomplishments and besides was very pretty. I was untidy and slow and was called 'dilatory' by my Great-Aunt Ellen, and had a mind that wandered. I was also plain. My school reports always had the note 'lacks concentration'. And yet I had two teachers whose teaching stayed with me, tall, elderly Miss McClyments who gave me an understanding of grammar and an appreciation for the pleasing sound of a sentence rightly in order. She read aloud for one hour on Friday afternoons. Miss Mitchell, who followed her, was regal and severe, but she encouraged us to use our eyes with our minds and to make a map with illustrations in watercolour of Stevenson's 'Inland Voyage'. She praised my effort, a rare occurrence.

Across the street from our house lived Mrs Hershberger who was an invalid. She had a Victrola and classical records. When she and her husband found that I loved to hear them, they would ask me to come in the evenings when Mr Hershberger would be home to put them on. So I heard Caruso, Galli-Curci, Kreisler, and many others who would transport me to heaven.

Another neighbour had a boarder, a tall, fair young man who was simply known as 'Mrs Bell's boarder'. I haunted that house to hear him play the piano; Brahms waltzes were his specialty. His name was James Hendel and he became my life-long friend. It might have been that he was pleased with my adoration of his performances, but in any case he was kind and amusing, and when I went to the Baldwin School, he wrote me a letter. These letters were to continue for seventy years. I addressed him as 'Mr H' and I was 'M. Shaw'. They would come when I was in want of understanding and help. The day I arrived at St Bride's School in Scotland, feeling the chill of being conspicuous with my accent and my clothes, there was a letter waiting for me, which said to look at this new experience as though it were a movie – not to let it penetrate, but to watch and enjoy it, and to look for the gold which we are told is to be found under the most unprepossessing exterior. This advice was to be my salvation.

My piano playing improved, always in six sharps or five flats, and when it was found that I could listen and then play the songs and dance tunes my sisters adored, I became of some value. My Aunt Elsie thought I should attend Miss Mollie Chaplin's Dancing Class, held in the ballroom of the Edgeworth Club. Being excessively shy, I found this an ordeal. I was among children of the private schools, the very well-to-do, and I had no one I knew. Aunt Elsie, the most generous and imaginative of persons, saw that I had proper dresses and slippers, but I felt a barn cat among Persians.

I felt that they all looked down on me and, for revenge, I took their bonnets, with ribbons and little pink roses tacked round them, and threw them up on a high cupboard. The next session, Miss Mollie lined us all up and then stood out in the middle of the floor and said, 'Now who threw the hats up on the cupboard?' I stood out and said, 'I did'. Nothing more was said at all, but one little boy came up to me afterwards and said, 'That was brave!'

Miss Mollie in her high white kid laced shoes and her marcelled hair with pince-nez on her neat nose was as light as thistle-down as she guided us in positions of posture and steps. I had one satisfaction. When we put on our ballet slippers, because I had an abnormally high arch with my first three toes the same length, I could stand on them with ease and had no need for a block. My feet were shaped like pieces of pie, and I had the nickname of 'Square Toes'.

Miss Mollie had a Mrs Porter who played the piano for our dancing and for when we marched around the room. She knew that I played by ear, and one day she said to me, 'Now you play the march for them to walk out.' So I did. Miss Mollie, then, meeting my sister Kay who came to pick me up, said, 'Your sister should have piano lessons.'

My sisters thought that since Caroline had had expensive lessons and had given them up, preferring to be a singer, that, as I could play well enough to amuse them, I had no need for lessons. And I, who had seen my friends labour with scales and silly little pieces, wanted none of it. But Martha thought of the organist at the Presbyterian church who played accompaniments for visiting singers. So Mr MacAfee was asked and I went in fear for my first lesson. He was a giant of a man with a head like a Roman Caesar. I found that I hadn't to learn these little pieces – 'Robin on the Bough' – but we began with simple duets, arranged by Josef

Low for teacher and pupil. Playing with Mr MacAfee helped me to read music, though I've never been proficient; people who play by ear always have difficulty in reading music. We progressed rapidly to lovely airs of Schubert and Mozart, to Weber's *Freischütz* and Polish folk songs. It was a joy for me to play.

My father died suddenly, and I had to find my way again. The house was sold, and we moved to an apartment nearby, the first of its kind in the village. Katharine became a bacteriologist for our Dr Nettleton. Martha had the hardest chore, not only bringing my sister Biddy and myself to the high standards and approval of the aunts, but cooking and keeping within the tiny income, for it was years before the estate was settled. Caroline fled to Glenshaw to live with our Great-Aunt Ellen, away from the scrutiny of relatives.

It was decided in 1918 by the aunts that I should go to boarding school, and from all the brochures it was the Baldwin School in Bryn Mawr that was chosen. This would be a preparation for the college of Bryn Mawr where two of my sisters had been. The eldest, Kay, had loved it and longed to have her younger sisters attend what she thought the finest college in the universe.

In summer the Baldwin School uniforms were of yellow linen with sailor collars; in winter they were the same design but of wool. I can still smell the lovely linen. Martha took me on the long train journey from Pittsburgh to Philadelphia, and I felt very smart in my first green skirt with a jacket that had a fur collar. The village of Bryn Mawr in autumn when the leaves are turning is a delight. I was happy to see such beauty, and the impressive huge school at the end of the long drive gave me no qualms. I was determined to enjoy – a habit which has been a fixture in my mind all my life.

We were met by the headmistress, a smiling but severe lady, and shown my room. Then I was introduced to a senior girl who was to be my guide in what books I would need, the classrooms, and who made me feel secure and wanted. That night I went to bed in a little room to myself feeling very satisfactory. But my entry into a classroom, which was made even more frightening by being filled with a dozen girls dressed like myself, and being confronted with algebra, chilled me to the marrow.

While I was at the Baldwin School, I continued my piano lessons with Miss Bertha Harding, who had managed to get home from Germany during the '14–'18 War. She loved Wagner and taught me the leitmotifs of the Ring. She also insisted that I go to hear the Philadelphia Orchestra. My greatest pleasure was hearing piano recitals by Rachmaninov, Gabrilovitsch, Percy Grainger and others.

With all my good intentions of trying hard to learn algebra and Latin, I nevertheless failed. It was suggested that I be tutored in both and then sent to a school offering individual attention. So I returned to Sewickley where a most serious young lady endeavoured to keep my mind on those two subjects all summer. I absorbed a little Latin because I liked it; with algebra, she wasted her time. My conscience hurt, with the miserable report from Baldwin and the sorrow of no return. I had a little comfort from having done well in English, and I knew that I had pleased my adored teacher, Bertha Harding, by my piano playing.

It was decided that I should go back to Bryn Mawr to the Misses Kirk's school, where my sisters Martha and Biddy had been, and where I would be welcome. It was in a private house, where most of the fifteen boarders were being prepared for Bryn Mawr College. Miss Abby Kirk was the headmistress, short and round, with thin white hair screwed into a bun; her fierce blue eyes and deep voice put fear in me. She taught Greek in the morning at the College. Her older sister, Miss Sophie, was tall, thin and fragile, with a sweet voice. She took me into her room when I arrived to welcome me warmly because of my two sisters, saying how diligent and outstanding they were, and how she and her sister Abby hoped to feel the same about me.

They didn't. It was soon realised that I was dilatory and needed discipline to make me concentrate. But there were happy times, because both Miss Kirks loved the theatre, and their pride among their friends were the Otis Skinners who lived nearby. At the school, Daisy Ashford's *Young Visitors* was turned into a play. I was Mr Salteena and wore Otis Skinner's top hat.

When I had left home for this new trial in education, I had a new blue felt hat, severe in shape, as was the style for schoolgirls, but it had a splendid addition. A family friend, a cowboy from Oklahoma, had arrived at Sewickley and had given me a rattlesnake hatband, complete with the rattle and a silver buckle. He had given me a treasure that made me feel superior in any gathering, and he promised to send me a present of a kangaroo lizard. This was forgotten in my long months of struggle to learn, but near the end of my days at Miss Kirk's, I received a large cardboard box with air holes. Inside were two kangaroo lizards, their names in delicate ink on their backs – Jake and Marian. Such shrieks and squeals resounded through the house as I allowed my friends to look at my rare present!

Miss Abby was alarmed and phoned the Professor of Zoology at Bryn Mawr. The box was too awkward to carry, so the lizards were put in a deep wastepaper basket with a screen on top. I followed Miss Abby through the streets of Bryn Mawr to the professor's house. The two suspects sat on their hunkers like kangaroos and stared. The professor viewed them with much interest and pronounced them innocent, not poisonous, and he doubted they would bite. He warned Miss Abby that they could make great leaps like their namesakes and had better be confined. So they lived in their box for the next few days. The kind chef tried to tempt them with many varieties of tit-bits, but they refused. We left together on the train for Sewickley, where they were given a pen, but they soon escaped. I hope they had some happiness.

In 1921 I returned from the Misses Kirk's school to the worry of my sisters about what they should do with me. The worry was relieved by a letter from Scotland. A minister friend of the family, the Revd Dr Hugh Hodge, had left America with his family to spend three years in Scotland to do temporary parochial work in

Glasgow and Edinburgh. They would like me to join them to go to a boarding school with their daughter for a year.

My guardian uncle, George Shaw, had to be consulted, and my aunts. There was enough money for the expenses, as the fees of the school in Scotland were only half those charged by the Bryn Mawr schools. I was thrilled beyond words. Then came my uncle's opinion that it was madness; my brother-in-law, Paul Caruthers, thought it would be dangerous, as he was certain there was going to be a war with Russia. Then a voice rose in my defence. A neighbour whom we called Aunt Tony Hartwell, who was from New York and had travelled in Europe, had a knowledge which was revered by the Shaw seniors. She said it was the chance of a lifetime and that I must go.

That summer was spent in exquisite anticipation. I was given new clothes, and I remember ironing my pyjamas, making creases down the legs, not knowing what was before me, but thrilled with the thought of seeing the ocean and a new country. A passage was booked for me on the *Columbia* sailing from New York to Glasgow on the eighth of September. Someone had to be found who was to travel on her, so that I could be put in her charge. The passenger list gave the name of a Mrs Brothers who lived in Pittsburgh. My aunt took me to call on her; we found she was a large lady with a mop of white curls and many gold teeth. I doubted her enthusiasm at taking on such a burden. She was obviously impressed by my aunt's chauffeur and her Pierce Arrow car. In the event, I hardly saw her for the entire voyage.

My sister Kay took me to New York, where we had breakfast with Uncle George, who gave me six gold sovereigns and warned me that they might be confiscated by the Customs when I landed, as the British had a rule then that no gold was to enter the country. I stuck them to the bottom of my cake of soap in its box.

I was delighted to see, when I went to go aboard, that the SS *Columbia* had three funnels though she was only 8,000 tons. I felt no fear.

The ship, which was of the Anchor Line of Glasgow, had a crew of Scots. Her captain was David W. Bone. My cabin companion was an elderly spinster, dry and stern. She was Scottish, as were most of the passengers. Her worry was that she could not buy a brush on board for her dentures. I had not heard the word 'dentures' before, and could not think what she meant. I could feel Miss N's disapproval of my exuberance and sensed that she thought I needed supervision.

The excitement was immense – being on the vast sea without sight of land, the dense fog off the Newfoundland Banks, then emerging into the bright sunlight with an iceberg nearby looking like a giant tent. We passed a four-masted schooner under full sail. Tiny Mother Carey's chickens (stormy petrels) flew between the waves in the strong wind. One of the crew brought me a large black and white bird that no one could identify. Years later I realised that it was a Manx Shearwater, often seen around Canna where I now live.

The first call was at Lough Foyle in the north of Ireland, for Londonderry. I remember watching a sailor at the stern taking soundings with a long thin rope to which a piece of lead pipe was attached, filled with tallow. He would haul it up and see what was attached to it. It was in the early hours of the morning, and pitch black. A searchlight was illuminating a small boat whose hold was filled with glistening fish, bright silver herring for our breakfast. As dawn came, there was the view of immaculate green fields divided into neat squares by stone walls, and the white cottages. The seagulls, which were floating about in the dark, were silent until the daylight, when they began their cries. Then we sailed along the Antrim coast, passing the Mull of Kintyre, and entering the estuary of the Clyde. We had reached Scotland.

There was a wait at what is called 'The Tail of the Bank' for a pilot to take the ship up the River Clyde to Glasgow. It was late afternoon, and as we slowly moved up the narrow river, we could see the shipyards on each side, with great hulls rising, swarming with men – the world-famous Clyde shipyards. Looking back to the west we could see thick black clouds with edges of bright gold.

We docked at Broomielaw, at the centre of the city, where the throngs of the steerage passengers and ourselves were massed to show our passports and visas. I was to be met, but there was no word of anyone. Captain Bone appeared to say that he would take me to the school that evening, as he lived in Helensburgh and his daughter was a pupil at St Bride's. There came the first feelings of fear: was I going to be thrown to the wolves? But a dapper man in a derby hat came to claim me, and I was pushed through the throng to find the Hodges. I first sighted their son Gilbert; I threw my arms around his neck, only to hear a gigantic policeman in a helmet yelling 'noon o' your cuddling here!'

Mrs Hodge, whom I called Aunt Annie, was the soul of love; we had a bond that stayed tight all through life. I had first to be fitted out with the school uniform, and then I was taken to tea to meet her step-mother, Mrs Beith, an elegant lady who lived in a mansion with maids in starched aprons and caps, who regarded me with interest as a strange creature. The tea was rich, with sandwiches and a great variety of little cakes; being greatly hungry I had one of each, to the amusement of the maid and Mrs Beith. They were not accustomed to someone who so much enjoyed their baking. Then came the train ride to Helensburgh, a pleasant town on the Firth of Clyde, and a drive in a horse cab up the hill to the school.

There was a main building with the boarders living in several very fine stone houses with large gardens planted with veronica and laurel and monkey puzzle trees. We had to ride bicycles because our house, Birk Hall, was some distance from the school. I was given a pair of brogues, and we had to wear black stockings and a green, very heavy gym tunic, and a black felt hat with a ribbon around it with the seal of St Bride.

I'd never known chilblains in my life before, but I suddenly found that my toes and heels were agony. One of my room-mates was a girl from the West Indies who was better off because she didn't have them on her feet; she could walk all right. But her hands – and she had beautiful hands – swelled and the knuckles discoloured, which made her weep with misery and shame. I could almost have shed tears in trying to get into those heavy brogues to ride the bicycle to school, and there seemed to be nothing to do about it. Everybody just took it for granted: of course you have chilblains; everybody has chilblains! But it was absolute torture.

The wonderful thing was my view from the window in the room which I shared with four other girls. It was a bow window, high up the hill. It looked across to Gourock and Greenock on the Clyde and I could see the ships come in, Atlantic liners, ships from India, and they all stood at the Tail of the Bank until they got a pilot who took them right up into Glasgow. We had to go for walks on certain afternoons in what they called 'crocs'; you walked two by two in your uniform. We were always taken by the domestic science teacher who lived in the house, obviously shy and not accustomed to the school any more than myself. I made it so that I very often walked with her and I would talk about Glenshaw and she would tell me about her father who had been engineer of a hospital ship in the War. There were wonderful roads then – no traffic – and we walked up what they called the Luss road. At the top of the hill, quite a long walk, if you looked into the distance, you could see a little glimpse of Loch Lomond and the wonderful hills, the Crianlarich hills. It was for me exciting and marvellous. There were also Highland cattle standing in deep bracken, which I'd never seen before.

Now the school was so anglified that there was nothing of Scotland in it at all, nothing of Scottish history, the clans, the Gaelic language – only the poets from Drummond to Burns and Walter Scott. But one day my heart was lifted by hearing the pipes being played. I looked out and saw in the back garden a tinker in his old army coat playing for pennies. I was thrilled and rushed down, going through the kitchen where I wasn't allowed, to give the tinker a penny, but the cook and the housemaid were so pleased to see that

that was what I liked. That was my first real taste of the Highlands, that tinker playing the pipes which I'd never heard before.

Then we had three recitals at the school, and to one of them came Mrs Kennedy-Fraser and her sister and her daughter, who played the harp. They were all three very elegant. Mrs Kennedy-Fraser had collected songs in the Hebrides, travelling with a theological student, Kenneth MacLeod, who took down the Gaelic words and later translated them for her. She composed elaborate accompaniments, converting them to art songs. At St Bride's, she talked about her visit to the Hebrides and then sang her songs, her sister accompanying. As a child, I had learned Scots songs and a few of Robert Burns', but these she sang were completely new. To think they'd been found in the Hebrides and I had never known anything about them! But there was something wrong, I felt; there was something more to these songs. If I could only go to those far-off islands and hear those singers myself!

Of all the teachers at St Bride's, I remember my French teacher best. She was from Aberdeenshire and was what would be called today a great Scottish Nationalist. She loved Scotland, and she told me afterwards how she had had her students make drawings to accompany the Arbroath Declaration of Independence, that wonderful statement that the earls and barons sent to Pope John, reminding him of his responsibility as the Father of Christendom to defend Scotland against England: 'So long as a hundred of us stand for our independence . . .' She had printed the Declaration and put it up with the drawings around her room, but the headmistress told her to take them down at once.

St Bride's was, scholastically, an extremely good school. I got a lot just from being there. I didn't pass in anything, but I learnt in spite of myself. What I got in that school was . . . well, two things. The headmistress, Miss Renton, taught the Old Testament, the minor prophets, and especially the Book of Amos, which have stayed with me all my life. Long years after, when my husband was very ill, I called on Miss Renton, then near ninety years. She was concerned about my problems and the difficulty of being in charge of the island. I reminded her that she used to scold me about my lack of concentration, but this had been my salvation. I couldn't keep my mind on how awful were my problems.

I had a marvellous piano teacher, Edgar Barrat, who was also a composer. He accompanied Kreisler and other soloists who came to Glasgow to play at St Andrew's Hall. He gave me my first Beethoven sonata, 'The Tempest', and more difficult things than I'd ever played – Chopin études for instance.

The school recital at the end of the year was the great event. There were eight of us to play and the first to perform was the girl who had won first prize in piano. After her followed a violinist who fainted and was carried off the stage past me, looking like a corpse. I had never seen anyone in a faint before, and when I had to mount the stage after her, my knees were shaking with fright. My Guardian Angel was responsible for my playing Chopin's First Prelude and the 'Butterfly' étude without a tremor. The headmistress came around and said, 'You must have a *special* prize!' That was Kipling's *The Years Between*, which I still have. It was a joy because I knew that, although I had done badly in my lessons, now at least I'd have something to show my sisters. I knew I had succeeded in what was really important for me.

At the end of school, Dr Hodge had taken a house at Boat of Garten, a village in Inverness-shire on the banks of the River Spey. In summer, this village was filled with professors, doctors of divinity and their families on holiday. Many were friends of the Hodges', among them Mr Frederick L. M. Moir, a brother-in-law of Mrs Hodge, whom I called 'Uncle Fred'. He and his brother John were famous African pioneers. When in their early twenties, they were inspired by David Livingstone to go to the hinterland beyond the coast of Portuguese East Africa, where they established trading stations and fought Arab slave traders. This was in the 1870s. Uncle Fred, with his flowing white beard, was still a monument of courage. When an angry bull appeared on the Boat of Garten golf course, sending the players flying into the Club House, he faced the bull with an umbrella, opening and shutting it to the astonishment of the bull, who then ambled off.

Being at the foot of the Cairngorm Mountains, we could enjoy hill climbing as well as long bicycle rides, one to Loch-an-Eilean (Loch of the Island) to see the nest of near-extinct osprey. There were many young people to enjoy these expeditions together, and we had dances in the barn beside our house, decorating the rafters with bunches of heather and bog-myrtle, the most delicious scent in Christendom.

Once we were asked to the nearby village of Carrbridge to a concert in their church hall, and it was here that I gave my first public performance. On the platform lit by an oil lamp was the piano, long out of tune, and many of the keys had lost their ivory covering. I played Chopin's 'Butterfly' étude, and this brought the minister who shared the platform to keep heavy time with his foot. He was joined by the congregation and it was a great success.

We left that happy house to take a paddle steamer at Inverness to travel down the Caledonian Canal. Now at the Sunday school in Sewickley seven years before, I had seen that among the prizes to be given for learning Bible verses was a magnificent edition of *Kidnapped*, complete with a map. I was determined to win that book so I learned a hundred and twenty Bible verses with the greatest difficulty, and I got the prize. As we passed Ballachulish, along Loch Linnhe where the Red Fox was murdered, I had my copy of *Kidnapped* with me to follow on the map. Uncle Hugh, seeing this, was very impressed. He opened the book and saw this inscription: 'To Margaret Fay Shaw, from the Reverend Hugh Lennox Hodge DD, for learning various parts of the Bible', and he said, 'Now let me hear you. What can you say?' And the only verse I could say was 'I am the true vine'.

That journey by MacBrayne paddle steamer took us across Scotland, through Loch Ness, the Caledonian Canal into Loch

Linnhe and on to Oban. Then south to Crinan where the tiny paddle steamer *Linnet* took us through that narrow canal to Ardrishaig where we joined the huge MacBrayne ferry, *Columba*, to sail up the Firth of Clyde, calling at Rothesay on the Isle of Bute and Gourock, and so to Glasgow where we boarded the SS *Cameronia*, bound for New York.

CHAPTER TWO

New York

IT HAD BEEN decided that I should study piano in New York: music, it seemed, was the only thing I could do. It was everybody's ambition to go to New York; all roads led there. My sister Kay, who was already trained as a pathologist, was enrolled in the New York University Medical School. It wasn't that I was to be under her wing – I had long since earned my independence – but it meant that I had a place to stay. Kay lived at the Studio Club, the famous YWCA for artists, in the annex where the residents included other kinds of students and where the rules were more relaxed. She had her own room because she had to study long hours, but we used to have Sunday suppers together. Kay would often bring things from the delicatessen, and I can remember thinking on one occasion how there must be something delicious in a paper bag, reaching in, and taking out human bones.

The Annex was a house on Madison Avenue, 694, which is still there, with two shops on either side of the entrance and you went up a flight of stairs in between, onto the two top floors where I and my friends lived who were all students of music, art or drama.

What joy to be young in New York during the 1920s! The brown-stone house on Madison Avenue resounded with violins, pianos and singing, high kicks and tap dancing. We came from every corner of the United States, from France, Poland and Cuba. Some were studying at the Art Students League where George Luks and Robert Henri ruled, and where the drawings in the life class were brought back for us to frown on.

There was a great deal of talent at the Studio Club. My room-mate, Frances Hutt, had been in the White Follies. I would accompany her when she sang Irish folk songs in the evening; her fiancé, also a singer, would sometimes join us: Thomas E. Dewey. Some of the girls, especially the ones on the stage, went far. What I found there, having been brought up to think that anyone on the stage is not quite nice, was that the girls on the stage were the most generous, the most moral, the very nicest. I'd left St Bride's, where I had to wear black woollen stockings and a gym tunic and a felt hat, a most unattractive uniform, to find I was sharing a room with a very pretty girl who had just come into the Club after a summer tour as the lead in the musical comedy, 'Irene.' She and her cousin practised high kicks and so on in the middle of the floor, and that was for me the beginning of a new era.

We had breakfast and dinner at night in the Club proper, round the corner on East 62nd Street. I was so shy and self-conscious when I went there, that if I couldn't walk into the dining-room with someone, I just wouldn't go; I went hungry. I couldn't bear to walk between tables with all those gaping girls, and it took me a long time to get over that.

Breakfasts and dinners were given in the Club, but for lunches and Sunday suppers we were on our own. Our search was for a cheap place to lunch; there were many pleasant little restaurants about us but usually beyond our means. One very snowy day we were told that a church down the street had lunches for twenty cents so we went with the hope of hot food. I wore a light tweed coat, for though the snow was deep, the sun was warm. I was met at the door by a lady wearing a Red Cross headdress who pinched my arm through my coat, asking if I had another. This riled me, and also the envelope that she gave me to open. It said on the outside 'GOD IS LOVE'. Inside it said: 'He who does not believe is in danger of Hell's fire.' It was a poor lunch, taken with hymns.

When spring came we would go to the delicatessen for a Swiss on rye sandwich and a dill pickle, then go to Central Park to sit on the warm boulders. If I had fifty cents I would treat myself to a turkey leg as well. The park was dilapidated, before Robert Moses restored it to great beauty, but it was safe to sit on those great boulders and enjoy.

I had started piano lessons with Oliver Denton. Since he had his own method, I began doing nothing but exercises all that winter. I was sent to his assistant, Mr Hall, until I was ready to learn proper pieces. When I went to Mr Denton, he would sit down in the chair, and take out his long cigarette holder and Russian cigarettes, and cross his knees and hold the music, and I had to play. And I had to memorise the music – we all did. Facility was easy, but sensitivity and a singing tone were all important. I had heard Myra Hess when I was at St Bride's and thought her playing marvellous, and when she gave her first recital in New York, Denton heard her and thought her superb. She had been taught by Mathay, who had much the same method as his.

It was from Constance McGlinchy, another Denton student, that I learned notation. At that time, I had perfect pitch; she taught me how to write down what I heard. And later when I got to South Uist, I was prepared to write down the tunes.

We heard a great deal of music and wonderful performances – Paderewski, Hoffman, Rachmaninov, Gabrilovitsch, Pachmann, Bauer, Godowski. Where will one hear such playing today? Then the New York Symphony under Walter Damrosch, before it merged with the New York Philharmonic. The children's concerts on Saturday mornings, when Ernest Schelling made his debut playing the celeste in the 'Nutcracker Suite.' What fun and delight it was.

We used to sit in the top gallery, especially for piano recitals, or for an orchestra concert, and there was one young man who used to sit with us, just a boy. His name was Munz, and he was so shabby and so poor! He had great long fingers and a long neck, and shaggy hair, and he was washing milk-bottles in the Sheffield Dairy at night to earn his way. In about two years' time we suddenly saw his photograph. He was making his debut, at the Town Hall, playing a tremendous programme, so we all went to hear him. He was dressed in a hired suit, and I remember we were quite near so that I could see that his socks were the thickest wool with a fuzz about an inch standing out. But he played beautifully, and went on from strength to strength. That was, of course, before the War, but I remember seeing his name after that, giving concerts. One thing he played was the César Franck Prelude, Chorale and Fugue. That's a hackneyed thing, and it is very easy to make it too sentimental, but he played it so well that I've never forgotten.

We had our own employment agency. If I had been a good sight-reader, I would have had beneficial and lucrative jobs, as did my pianist friends, who were hired to accompany singers in their practicing. One friend played for a callisthenics lady who had a class for men who wanted to reduce and renew their agility. They were told to lie on the floor and pretend they were seals.

I was given various little jobs to earn small wages. I refused to take dogs out, but I could serve as the club telephone operator, getting the lines so entangled that I would pull out all the plugs, hoping they would call back. I could also run the elevator. Looking after children in an elegant apartment while the mother attended the Philharmonic gave me my first feelings of injustice, as I felt that I should have the ticket while she watched her children. The best paying job was touching up an advertisement for a tailor: I had to paint ermine tails on pictures of the collar of a smart coat, and there were four hundred to do most carefully. They had to reach the tailor by six o'clock and I worked furiously to finish. It was after six when I ran to the subway to go down town to his office. An irate old man opened the door to say I was too late. But a young man appeared at his shoulder and took pity on me. I was given the $4.50 I had earned.

It is surprising how money adds up, even though it was coming in at only thirty-five cents an hour. Sometimes it was fifty; I even earned a dollar as a waitress for a banquet at the Art Students League. New York was a wonderful place! Anybody with the least talent who would work could always get on, generally with menial jobs, but the person who employed them was usually sympathetic and wanted to help.

One job was at the Hackett Gallery where I addressed envelopes and helped at the exhibitions. John Keating arrived from Ireland for his, a small dark man, shy and silent, in a high-necked blue jersey, like his splendid paintings of the men of Aran. What a contrast to the gathering of arty New Yorkers chattering and refilling their glasses of spiked punch.

The best job I had was ushering Friday afternoons and Sunday evenings at Carnegie Hall. I could come back alone after midnight, walking along Fifty-seventh Street to Fifth Avenue, over to Madison, absolutely unafraid. Almost every Thursday night, a friend would take me to the concert and I would often hear the programme again on Friday afternoon. Toscanini was at that time the conductor of the New York Philharmonic, and anyone who ever heard Toscanini knows you never hear his equal; nobody ever surpasses.

I had the second-tier boxes. You were given a little key to open the box when the boxholders arrived, and if they left the box, you had to open the door again to let them back in. I used to arrange it that I would let down the little window in the door, so that I could hear. This was all right, until one evening a very grand lady arrived, climbing up the stairs like a black galleon, with a black satin cape and an enormous black hat, with loads of necklaces and one thing or another. And she looked at this door and she looked at me, and she said, 'My name is Mrs Henry Fairfield-Osborn. I own this box. I will *not* sit in a draught! Shut it at once!' So I shut it at once.

Another time there appeared a very sweet-looking girl, with her young man. They had with them eight blind girls, taking them to hear the concert. There weren't enough chairs in the box, so I hunted around and got other little folding chairs. The young man was extremely grateful and gave me a quarter. And I said, 'Oh, no, no, no thank you.' 'Please take it!' So I took the quarter, and that was my first tip! The second (and the last) was on a Sunday night. An order of brush makers had hired the hall for a big meeting. They occupied all the boxes, all seemed short men, all with black bushy beards, like their brushes, and all kept their black hats on. They kept coming in and out to visit each other, and every time they went out and let the door shut to go in another box, I had to unlock the doors – back and forth, back and forth, very busy. When it came to the end of the evening, I saw all these little black hats crowded together, and then one came forward and gave me ten dimes!

At that time we used to go on Sundays, very occasionally when we had some money, away down Second Avenue to about Tenth Street, to a restaurant called 'The Russian Bear'. The chef was said to have come from a famous restaurant in Moscow; he probably did, because the patrons were all Russian emigrés. There was a balalaika orchestra that played wonderfully, and we used to have bortsch soup with masses of sour cream on it, wonderful food. They got to know us and used to play our favourite Russian songs. Once, we saw that a Russian folk singer, Plevitskaya, was giving a concert in the Town Hall, and we went. She was a great big strapping woman, wearing Russian costume, and who accompanied her but our orchestra from 'The Russian Bear'! She had a tremendous, deep, glorious voice, and her audience was thrilled. Soon after that she gave another concert, and this time Rachmaninov accompanied her.

Even then, in those years, I was interested in folk-music. I loved to accompany one singer who sang Irish and old Scots songs, and I'd had a taste of Gaelic songs ever since hearing Mrs Kennedy-Fraser at St Bride's. Now along Lexington Avenue there was an Irish bookshop which I haunted because they had books on Ireland and on the Irish language. And they had gramophone records of Irish songs. (The treasure I have to this day is Lennox Robinson's book of Irish poetry – the best of its kind.) Miss Slattery, who was head of the Irish bookshop, and a Mr Ferrand were very long-suffering with me. I used to love to go in there and talk to them and listen to the records, and I also went for their Irish evenings of folk-dancing.

Uncle George sent me one hundred dollars, which was supposed to be for essential things, but I spent seventy-five of it on a small harp, an Irish harp made by Lyon and Healey in Rochester, New York. They're not as big as a clarsach, the Scottish harp which you put on a stool in front of you. This Irish one you play in your lap, to accompany singing. Everybody was horrified at the expense and at the fact that I couldn't play it. Eventually I could, and this little harp was part of my baggage when I went to Paris and to the Hebrides.

There was another bookshop on Madison Avenue kept by an elderly Scotsman with a walrus moustache. I would wander in, looking for books about Scotland. I told him that I had been there the year before, and that I was interested in Gaelic. I bought two little volumes one afternoon, and when I left the shop and started walking up Madison Avenue, a man who'd been in there caught up to me and said, 'Pardon me, I hear you're interested in Gaelic. I have a friend who has a great knowledge of Gaelic, and he would very much like to meet you. He's the chief of Clan Fergus of Strachur, and if you will wait here, I will go into this drugstore and phone him, to see if we could arrange a meeting. My name is Lemon and I come from Ireland, myself.'

So I waited and he went in and he came back and said, 'Yes, the chief of Clan Fergus will phone you.' So I told him where I lived and that was that. The next morning I had a phone call to say that it was the chief of Clan Fergus who was speaking and that he would like to come and call, so I said, 'Well, come this afternoon; perhaps you could come to tea.' Oh, yes, he would. At teatime, the girl at the switchboard rang me and I could tell from her voice that something was up. 'The chief of Clan Fergus is here to see you!' I hurried across Madison Avenue and along 62nd Street to the Club and went in, and I saw in the lounge such a vision that I almost went out again. The chief of Clan Fergus was a tall man, wearing a kilt and a sort of military jacket and a great leather belt with a very handsome silver buckle. He had a bonnet with eagle-feathers and a dirk in his stocking. His cape was thrown open, and his hair hung in rat-tails around his collar.

However, I went up and spoke to him, thinking 'how in the ——— will I ever get you across Madison Avenue with everybody looking?' At that time, you never saw a kilted Highlander. I had told a friend, whose parents had come from Fife, that she must come and help me serve tea. She told her other friends that I was expecting this Highlander, this chief of Clan Fergus, so they were all at the windows looking down on Madison Avenue as I walked with the chief across the street. The trolley-cars slowed down; everybody gaped, my face felt so hot, but I got up the stairs at last.

Our house-mother Mrs Morris said, 'Oh, this is very nice indeed, Margaret, and you can have my sitting-room.' So we took him in there, and when Janet Robertson appeared, she could hardly keep from giggling aloud. I had a little primus stove, and we got the kettle to boil, and we made a cup of tea, and Janet was whispering in my ear, a voice you could hear across the street, 'His hair's dyed! Look at the purple gleam!' I had bought, I remember, six macaroons, and I also had bought milk. Now all these things cost me money, of which I was very short. When I produced the macaroons, he said: 'Haven't you anything plainer than this?' I said, no, that that was all I had. 'And I don't take milk,' he said, 'I would like lemon.' Well, my room-mate had a piece of lemon in a saucer; it had been in the window for some days, and it was covered with soot. But I washed it off and brought it on a saucer.

Then he asked what I had in the way of Gaelic books. Well, I had the first volume of Mrs Kennedy-Fraser's songs, and I had a grammar, and I had the Columba Collection of Gaelic songs, and he said he'd like to see them, so I brought them forth. He sat down beside me on the little settee, and he ran his long finger under the Gaelic words, translating them aloud, which he could perfectly well do because the English was written underneath. They were all very sentimental love-songs, which of course made me want to giggle more than ever, and I could hardly contain myself, and this went on and on and on. And then he said that he would like to borrow the grammar and the Columba book of Gaelic songs and would certainly send them back.

By this time it was very dark and snowing hard. When he looked out the window and saw the snow falling, he took his rat-tails and made them into a little bun at the back of his neck, and slipped his bonnet over them, and flung his great cape around him, and stalked out.

I didn't hear from the chief of Clan Fergus for months, so I wrote him and said would he please send back my grammar and my book of Gaelic songs. He then phoned and said that he would like to come to tea. Now Mrs Morris was very cute and could lie for you very easily; she said, 'Margaret has got a very sore throat; we think it might be tonsilitis. She can't see anyone, but she would like the books back!' Still they didn't come. So I sent him stamps, and a piece of brown paper and string in a manilla envelope, and said to please return them, and he did.

During this time, I met a young woman, Heloise Russell-Ferguson, who was giving concerts of Mrs Kennedy-Fraser's songs, accompanying herself on a harp. She was thrilled to meet the man she took to be the chief of her clan and told him she hoped he would come to the concert. And so he did, but then she got the bill for the box he had taken!

I heard afterwards that he was extremely mean, though he lived in the Explorer's Club. He told me that he had been on the Macmillan expedition, that he had been soldiering in Mesopotamia and Egypt, that he knew the world. He told me his mother was Polish, a Sobieski, and was connected with the House of Stuart. He could show me, to prove his identity, a letter from the Duke of Argyll. Everybody in New York believed him to be the chief of Clan Fergus of Strachur and he was most popular with the Scottish societies.

CHAPTER THREE

From Plymouth to Portree and Stornoway, Oxford, London, Paris, Dublin

I WAS LONGING to get back to Scotland; with the part-time jobs, I eventually got enough to go. At that time, Henry Luce and another man at Yale University started the first tours for students. I decided to go with my friend Isobel Conkline, the daughter of a famous professor at Princeton, and a friend of hers who was with her at Smith College and whose father was Dean at Princeton, Catherine Gauss. Another friend decided that she would join us for a little while, so we four shared a cabin. The little money we had we pinned into the pockets of our jackets. It was an old Dutch ship, and the steerage – so-called 'tourist class' – was filled with college students and university professors. It was primitive, but it was all right; we thought it was great fun.

I had made out the whole itinerary. We were to land at Plymouth, and we were to see Clovelly and the north coast of Devon. We were to see Exeter and the cathedral, and then we were to go on to Oxford, where I had a friend much older than myself, whose husband was a Fellow at Balliol. We could find some place to stay at Oxford and there we would get our bicycles. When we got ashore at Plymouth, I was the boss. I was then nineteen and I knew everything. I said, 'Now, this is where Drake played bowls. You see that place? And this is also famous for Devonshire cream, so that's what we'll do in the morning.'

We arrived quite late at night and had no accommodation, so the station-master said, 'Now, I'm going to lock you in, but you're quite safe here, and in the morning we'll let you out and you can take your train.' We had to sleep on the benches in our clothes, which was very uncomfortable because the benches were sloped and they had a hole at the back that your elbow went through. I was awakened in the morning by a gentleman in his braces, a sweeper with a brush in one hand, handing me my handbag which he had found while sweeping out the ladies' room. I didn't admit this to the others, who were still asleep.

We went out for breakfast, but nothing was open except a little dairy place that sold cream and milk and butter. They said that they'd give us a cup of tea and some Devonshire cream which we ate with a spoon, feeling very ill afterwards. It was much too early to get on the train, but Gaussie (as we called her) said that she'd watch the bags while we went to see where Drake played bowls. So we hurried off, first to cash a cheque at Thomas Cook's, and then to find a green, which I supposed was the place, and then we hurried back again. To our dismay, when we entered the station, we saw our bags on the platform at various intervals and Gaussie at the far end looking furious. We'd missed the train, and two very nice ladies in the train had helped her to get out and had thrown the bags after her! However there was a train later in the day, so we caught that, and went on our way.

In Oxford we three got our bicycles, and when a much older friend arrived on the scene, Peggy Hitchcock and her new husband David, she said we could go with them on their bicycle tour to Broadway and Kenilworth and Warwick, which we did. Gloucestershire is very hilly, it was all up and down. The old bicycle I had was much too high, and the handles had the brakes you squeeze. When we got to the top of a hill where you ride down into Broadway, I started off, we all did, and then my brakes gave way. I went on past the others, and God just fared me down, round the bends, and here and there, and I went right straight through

Broadway and never stopped till I was well on the other side of the village going up another hill! They were all very much alarmed and thought they'd find me on the roadside, but not at all.

We cycled through the Lake District, and we were at Windermere – at Oxford we were filled with Matthew Arnold and at Windermere we were filled with Wordsworth. Then we had an awfully long way to go to Carlisle, because I was determined to see the Roman Wall. We had to walk up the Kirkstone Pass, pushing our bicycles. I remember walking backwards to rest my knees, in order to get up there in time to get a funny little bus that would take us and our bicycles till we could get another straight road into Carlisle.

Eventually, we found our way to the Wall. I remember we passed by a lovely rectory. It was Sunday, just at lunchtime, and we could smell the rector's lunch cooking. He was out in the garden in a straw hat, and when we said that we were looking for the Wall, he directed us and said we might notice that the house and the church had Roman stones in them. We were hoping that he'd invite us in and give us a cup of tea, but nothing doing. So we rode a long way, a wonderful ride because there was nothing on the roads. We got as far as a place called Denton-on-the-Wall, and then we returned to Carlisle and put our bikes on the train to Glasgow.

Out of Helensburgh, we took the Ness Road which I knew so well as a schoolgirl, when I walked 'in croc'. This was wonderful, to be free and riding bicycles! And we got eventually to Ardlui, where we spent the night in a miserable bedroom in an awful old iron bed. A framed motto above it read: 'Cast your burden on the Lord, and He will sustain you.'

Now the next day we started for Crianlarich, and it poured and it rained. We used to say, our noses and everything running with water, 'Smell the pines!' and that would draw everything up! We spent the night at Crianlarich in a cottage. We couldn't afford to eat in the dining-room, but there was a hut outside the hotel where they had afternoon teas. Parked outside this shed was a huge limousine, with a little fence around the top, the baggage tied on. A chauffeur in dark-green livery was leaning up against the door of this little tea-place. Inside, we noticed at the next table an elderly man and his wife – Americans. He had white hair, and enormous tortoiseshell-rimmed glasses. He was so busy watching us that he couldn't even eat. At last he could restrain himself no longer: 'Where're you two girls from?' We said that we were from America. 'The States?' 'Yes.' 'So'm I,' he said. 'Isn't it nice to come in here and have this piece of gingerbread? I hired this here car at Southampton. Drove all the way up here and ain't seen nuthin' but mutton and tombs!'

Going down the road in Glencoe, Isobel had a flat tyre, and she tried to ride lightly and not sit on the seat or anything to save the tyre, but at last she had to get off in case she ruined it. We had to walk for miles until we reached Ballachulish where they mended the tyre for us. We cycled up to Fort William and up the Great Glen. When we got to Inverness, so wet and so dirty and tired, Mrs McKenzie, the lady we were staying with, said, 'Now, you give me your pullovers and that.' And I remember that I had nothing else to put on; I had to put on my pyjamas and go to bed. But she washed all our things and dried them so that in the morning we could start off all clean and dry for Strome Ferry.

The hotel there was a great tall house, almost like a keep. It was run by the most terrible old woman that I've ever seen in my life. She must have had a wig, but anyway it was grey, and filled with cobwebs and fluff. Her husband had the ferry across Loch Carron to Kyle of Lochalsh. When he saw that there were just the three of us, he didn't want to make the effort, and of course he would get the money if we stayed over. So we had to spend the night in that awful, smelly hotel. I remember we felt that this woman looked like someone who could hit you on the head. Then suddenly, very late at night, there was a commotion. A very smart car had arrived with three elegant county ladies in it, but he wouldn't take them across, no matter how hard they begged, so they had to spend the night too. I could hear them shouting for hot water and dry sheets, because the place was damp; they were making a great fuss!

The next morning we did get across to Kyle where I'd already written from New York to engage a room. I'd never been to Skye, I didn't know anything about this country, except, as I say, from the map. I'd seen a name in large print, among all the other names, called Monkstad, up north of Portree. Well, I thought, that looks bigger than Portree. I'll write to the post-master and ask if there's a minister in the town who would know of anybody who would take us in. So I sent two letters off, one to Portree and one to Monkstad, asking for information about accommodation and saying I was interested in folk-music and folk-dancing. The answer came from Monkstad: 'As for your interest in folk-music and folk-dancing, my message in this world is to entreat souls to flee from the wrath to come. And let me counsel you not to touch a musical instrument or correspond on the Lord's Day.' The other letter from Portree was from a seceder. I'd said to him that we liked kippers and we didn't mind rain. He wrote that he knew of a Mrs Matheson who would be sure to take us in, and that kippers and rain were a very good combination for the inner and outer man, and he hoped we'd go to see him, which we did. And he was a dear, an awfully nice man.

So, we arrived at Kyle to get the steamer – all this was before us. The bank agent had never seen Americans, or certainly not on bicycles. He was so fascinated that he took ages to cash our travellers' cheques, asking us a thousand questions, and we kept saying, 'Now, we've got to go!' We were dying to get to Portree, where we would have letters. 'Yes,' he said, 'but I'd like to know . . .' And suddenly there was a toooot! And I said, 'That's the steamer! The steamer's going!' 'Yes, yes, but you'll have another tomorrow.'

So we got to Skye, and to Mrs Matheson, who lived with her fierce old mother-in-law and her husband, a butcher. Now at that time I was very anxious to hear real Gaelic songs and she said, 'Well, I can tell you someone to hear, and I'll ask him to come to the house.

He's crippled, he's in a wheelchair, so it's very difficult for him to get about.' So Hector Kelly, who lived some miles up the road, was asked to come in. He was a great heavy young man and we had an awful time getting him up the stair to the little sitting-room. He had a wonderful voice, and wonderful songs, and he sang verses in eight lines, called *oran mor*, what you would call classical songs, and yet very fine. He asked us to come out to Braes, so we spent the day with him and his sister and heard more songs.

I had carried a heavy book entitled *Hebridean Memories* by Seton Gordon F.Z.S. Looking from our window one day, I saw a tall distinguished man in a kilt and blue bonnet walking along the street. Our landlady told me it was Seton Gordon and that he was very friendly, and she was sure he would like to meet us. So a note to say how much I had enjoyed his book brought an invitation to tea. I knew that he was a piper and asked him to play. He demonstrated how, in tuning his pipes, he would play short airs to bring the drones to the exact pitch. He then played a pibroch called 'The Battle of the Pass of Crieff'. I was in ecstasies, though it was hard on the ears of the other guests who had not heard the pipes inside a house.

The month or more we were there we made great friends with people in Portree – friends to this day. We rode all over Skye, carrying everything on the back of the bicycles, but every time that we would go any place and get far from home, a pedal would come off, or a tyre would go, because they were second-hand bikes, long-used. They were much too high for me with my short legs; it was an awful business pushing them.

We heard that there was going to be an excursion to Stornoway, to go up and come back the same day. This was wonderful, to see the Outer Isles and off we went. They had a piper on board and a lot of drunks. We got to Stornoway in a deluge! It was impossible to do or see anything. We went up to 'The Castle', a Victorian pile built by the previous owner of Lewis, a Colonel Matheson. It had a conservatory, with plants and with orange trees in tubs, which amazed us, as we expected a town with fishing boats and not this elegance. However, the glass roof leaked on us; a reverend gentleman sat in silence under his umbrella.

It was a great opening for me to hear Gaelic, and when the Provost of Portree, who was a Mr MacKinnon, heard from Mr Matheson in the butcher shop that there was an American who was anxious to hear songs and would like to know Gaelic, he sent me MacAlpine's Dictionary and a book of Gaelic stories and prose writings, far too difficult for me to read but it gave me a taste; it was a beginning. And then Mrs Matheson would always speak to us in Gaelic, and she had nicknames for us. We wanted to hear a Gaelic service, so we went to church with her; it was hours long. Mrs Matheson put her hand in her little jacket pocket and took out what I call 'Presbyterian drops', known in Scotland as 'pandrops,' big white peppermints, hard round things, and gave us each one to sustain us. When the dominie saw that there were English-speaking guests in his congregation, he gave a whole long sermon in English as well!

After a lunch of hot boiled potatoes and cold mutton, we went out on this lovely afternoon for a walk to pick heather. When we got back, we were met at the street door – you walked in from the street and went up a flight of stairs into the living-quarters – by Mrs Matheson, who grabbed our heather and stuck it behind the hat rack as quick as possible. The great big feet and the long black skirt of her mother-in-law were just seen descending the stairs, and Mrs Matheson said – the old mother didn't speak any English, only Gaelic – 'Now, I don't mind, myself, but my mother-in-law wouldn't like it at all, if you would pick flowers on the Sunday!'

Now, during our visit there was a Communion which began on the Thursday and lasted till Monday. On Sunday, people came from the island of Raasay and from all over Skye, in pony-traps and by boat. And they filled a huge open field. They sang psalms, in Gaelic, this huge congregation, out in the open air! The precentor would chant a line, because the people couldn't read; he would chant the line, and the whole congregation would then answer, singing. He then chanted the next line, and they sang on and on – the whole great volume!

The memory of my journey to Skye, hearing the authentic Gaelic songs, stayed with me the following two years in New York. I was determined to return to the Outer Hebrides, so with the help of a small legacy and accompanied by a friend, Dorothy Kurtz, I set out in the summer of 1926. We sailed with our bicycles from Oban to Barra. Barra's port, Castlebay, was busy with a large fleet of herring boats, the harbour dominated by Kismul Castle, once the stronghold of the chief of the MacNeills. John MacPherson, a famous story-teller known as 'The Coddy' and the most important man on Barra, found a sail boat to take Dot and me to Eriskay, the next island to the north, and lent me a map of the Hebrides.

Eriskay at that time had a fine church with the priest's house attached, a school house, and a shop, all of which were slated; all the cottages were thatched. The island would have looked the same to Charles Edward Stuart who landed there from France in 1745. It was Eriskay where he first set foot on the soil of Scotland, of which he hoped to be king. There were no roads on the island – only paths – and no means of transport other than small ponies.

Then there was a short crossing to South Uist, where we could mount our bikes on a good road and travel north – on our left, the machair, green grazing land at the edge of the Atlantic where a beach of white sand stretched the entire length of the island – twenty-two miles. On the right was the contrast of low bog, lochs, and rough ground to the high range of hills. A cart took us across the half-mile ford from Uist to Benbecula, and with the rising tide the two-wheeled cart filled with water. The horse had to swim a few strokes, and myself sitting in the rear tried to keep our bikes upright with our luggage bags tied on. I was soaked.

Benbecula was a contrast. A small island – five miles square – it was low-lying and rich pasture and, compared to what we had been seeing, prosperous. Then the rain descended: it rained all across Benbecula and we had to bike with strong winds against us. Again, a four-mile ford to cross in a cart threading its way carefully by markers in order to avoid quicksand. We could see nothing of North Uist which looked to be the most desolate land on earth. Stopping at a little shop, the only things we found to buy were thin white biscuits which melted into paste as we cowered against a wall. The shop keeper regarded us, pulling aside the lace curtain of the shop window.

From North Uist we sailed to Rodel at the south end of Harris, where we stayed in a large house that had been the shooting lodge of the Earls of Dunmore but was now an hotel. We were able to dry out and to see the beautiful little church of St Clement's. The date of its foundation is unknown, but it was completed in the early sixteenth century. It has recessed tombs with splendid carvings which show the power and culture of the MacLeods of that time.

Harris is composed of mountains and we began our long journey up the steepest road, pushing our bicycles only to find at the top that to ride down would soon wear out our handbrakes. We passed many little heaps of stones and were told that these were coffin cairns. Men carrying a coffin on their shoulders would rest by the road and add a stone with a prayer. At the village of Tarbert, there was a whaling station where we could see whales on the wharf being skinned, and the stench was indescribable on that hot day; as we again had to push our bikes up the longest and steepest hill, that aroma stayed with us for miles. At last we made the long descent into Lewis and had a reasonable ride to the town of Stornoway, the most important town and port in all the Hebrides. I was worried as we were riding into town on a Sunday, for the Lewis people are strict Sabbatarians. But we came to a small temperance hotel where the owner, a Miss MacKenzie, welcomed us, only concerned about our being tired and hungry.

Our aim was to reach the Butt of Lewis, the furthest point, and the road took us by the Callanish Stones. Only Stonehenge can equal them, but there is nothing to compare with the site. On a high green field are near forty-eight standing stones in a cruciform. Little drifts of mist were blowing across from the sea – the perfect place for listening to Stravinsky's 'Rites of Spring'. Nearby were other stone circles and a Pictish broch with hollow walls and narrow little steps, which appeared to me to be built by, and for, small, thin people.

When we reached the end of the road, we found that we had a long walk across the fields to the lighthouse at the Butt of Lewis. It was nearly dark when we reached our goal. Then back to a kind lady who took us in for the night, and back to Stornoway the following day to take the ship to the mainland, and the train to London.

My intention was to continue with the piano, and what I wanted most of all was to study with Myra Hess. I had written to her in London, asking if I could study with her because I would love to be able to produce just one note the way she played. She answered and said yes: 'Come and I will help you "produce that note".' I found when I got to London that she was on tour, so there was no chance. But I had another name. A man I'd met in New York at the 42nd Street Library had said to me that one York Bowen was a very good teacher. So I arranged to go into London from Oxford, where I'd gone to stay with Dolly MacGregor,

York Bowen thought I'd been badly trained. His studio was above a funeral shop with a window full of *immortelles* – in Baker Street (and of course I thought of Sherlock Holmes). I opened the door and here was a man with a very pink, fat, wide face and fair-to-grey hair, brushed back. He had puffy, pinky hands and a gray alpaca jacket. As soon as I played for him, I could feel his disgust. He gave me a Brahms scherzo, very hard to play and completely against my sort of taste or feel, and I was told to practice this and come back. He had classes and people performing once a week, and he expected me to come in from Oxford and then go back in the evening. It was too expensive for me – I had very little money – and also it wasn't any fun to go back late at night. So, after a few weeks, I said I just wouldn't come and that was the end of the lessons. And he said, 'Well, that's the way it is with Americans.'

I had a strong taste of Oxford, living with the MacGregors. Dolly's husband, Duncan, was a Fellow of Balliol. He would take me for long walks in the country. Sometimes we'd take a bus out a way and then walk, stopping at a pub for sandwiches. I learned to drink beer. 'You musn't *sip* it; you must drink it.'

The wives of the dons who came to play bridge with Dolly were dull and snobbish. I was continually cold. At the back of the house was a little garden which opened out onto the playing fields of Balliol. The mists rose and came in through the open French windows. I had to practice in a hired room where there was a blue gas fire that smelt, but it was still cold and my hands and arms began to ache. I had my theory lessons in a warm drawing-room with Mr Alchin, a kind, patient man, and even the trips down to London for the lessons with the unpleasant Mr Bowen were welcome because the train was warm!

I kept trying to find somebody who could teach me about the modes – how to identify them. Friends of Dolly's said, 'You must meet Foxie.' That was Fox-Strangeways who did the great study of Indian music. He wrote me that the one I should meet was Martin Freeman who had collected Irish folk songs. Eventually we did meet, he came to Barra and to Canna to visit and taught me then to recognise the modes.

My happiest memory is of Joyce Cary. Dolly would take me over to visit when she and Gertie Cary would go to choir practice – they both sang in the Bach Choir. Joyce had come back from Nigeria, where he'd written short stories for *The Saturday Evening Post*, and he was now writing a novel. Time was passing and they were living on very little – though they had a nursery maid for their four little boys. But of course he did go on and had great success, first with *The African Witch*, and others which were very popular in America. He didn't tell me about Africa but, rather, about literary figures he'd known – Middleton Murry and Katherine Mansfield, for instance. I told him about South Uist, and he said I should write a novel about it. On the back of one of my photographs of Mingulay, he wrote four or five titles of novels I should read to get an idea of how you construct one. By the time I sent him my South Uist book, he had advanced muscular dystrophy – only two fingers would work and his arm was in a sling – but he wrote me a note: 'Dear Meg, You've made a beautiful book.' I'm glad that he could see that I did make something out of South Uist after all.

Though the friends and the lessons in music theory with the kind and patient Mr Alchin were hard to leave, the intense cold made my elbows and wrists increasingly sore and Paris, I thought, would surely be warmer; I could continue lessons there. My sister Biddy was even more anxious to go as she was not able to adjust to English ways. We crossed third class from Newhaven to Le Havre and I had such a cold that I could hardly breathe. A sailor, seeing me on a hard bench with a resounding wheeze, covered me with a blanket.

Our first night was spent in a small hotel near the Gare Montparnasse. Since we arrived early in the morning, a room was not ready, but I begged for a bed and we were given a room where the bed was obviously just vacated. To my sister's horror, I fell into it and pulled the covers over my head. The lovely warmth and a soft pillow put me to sleep and I woke in the dark to feel free of wheeze and with only a snuffle. Biddy had been given a proper room but though hungry was afraid to go out into this wicked city alone to find a restaurant.

Next day she had made arrangements to go temporarily to the University Club, for which I was not eligible. I had the misfortune to find a hotel which appeared to be of near elegance, though a modest price. My room was on the very top floor, about seven flights, and I had my little harp in its harp-case to lug up, and baggage. I was in a bare room with one light bulb hanging in the centre of the ceiling. The room had a wash-hand basin, however, with cold water.

I went to bed and woke up in the night, feeling very hot and very restless, and my face felt so sore that I got up and turned on the light and looked in the mirror. My face was scarlet. I rinsed it in cold water whereupon all these bumps came up. I thought at once 'Bed bugs!' I pulled back the sheet and they ran in all directions. So I sat on a little chair in the window, and looked down on the crossing of the Montparnasse and Raspail Boulevards. The Beaux Arts were having a ball, a celebration, and they were all in costume, and the band was playing and they were dancing in the street.

I stood it until I was just about dropping off; I couldn't stay awake, so I took the top bedclothes off the bed and just left the sheet on it, and left the light on because bed bugs won't come out in the light. I greased my feet and hands with Vaseline, and tied my pyjama legs tight and lay on top of the bed. Though I was cold without having any covers, I lay there until morning. Then I descended the long flight of stairs to meet the concierge, who was a great big man with an enormous walrus moustache, in a frock coat. I said: '*Monsieur, beaucoup des animaux dans mon lit!*' He replied, pointing his fingers like a schoolmaster, '*Bêtes Mademoiselle, bêtes!*', showing a real concern for the purity of the French language. He said I would be all right after that night, that he would see that I had somewhere else to sleep, that they would soon do away with the bed-bugs.

I was away all day and when I came back, I found the room sealed with paper, with formaldehyde candles burning inside. I was given a tiny room just big enough to have a little bed in it, but there was no window except for an opening above the vent for all the WCs of the hotel; it was very unpleasant. But the next night, the concierge said that the room was quite all right. The smell of the formaldehyde was so strong, I think that was what gave me a sound sleep; however, the next night, the bed bugs were back again! I moved next day to the Pension Jeanne at 14 Rue Stanislas.

Later on, when I was living in South Uist, I told this story to Peigi and Mairi MacRae and to Angus John Campbell. One of them said that the sailors who were sailing on the freighters had this trouble, especially with the Runciman Line, and that a Uist man had made a nice song about the bed bugs. I said, 'I must get that song.' Mairi MacRae said, 'It's a very nice song! It's a very nice song!'

The excitement of being in Paris, the thrill of the ballet! Satie's 'Les Matelots' and Lifar in 'Le Chat'; 'Les Folies Bergeres', with Josephine Baker wearing a tail of brilliant feathers, dancing like a ribbon in the wind, with her sweet silver voice. Just around the corner from Rue Stanislas was Le Dome where we would have coffee at night and watch the celebrities gathered there. The artist Fougita with a lady who wore a little live green chameleon tethered to her lapel with a tiny chain.

I had French lessons from Mademoiselle Delcaire who coached the members of the Comédie Française. She liked to have our lessons in a small café, which pleased me. I was fortunate in having such an interesting and warm friend as a teacher, but she shocked me one day by saying that if there should be another war, the Boches would conquer France. How right she was.

One day a friend and I hired bicycles to ride out in the country to a restaurant called Le Petit Robinson. There we ascended trees to a platform and our luncheon was delivered up in baskets. We had a fine view of the balloon field nearby. When we returned it was at the busiest time of traffic. We put our bikes on the Métro at Port Royale, thinking we would arrive near where we had hired them, but when we arrived there were no bikes: they had been held at Port Royale. So we had to return to pick them up and ride them back. I was so frightened that I rode in the grassy island in the centre of the roaring boulevard. A policeman ordered me off, but when I explained my fear he allowed me to continue. I thanked him for my life.

I had music lessons from Katherine Wolff, a friend from my New York years. She had become an assistant to Nadia Boulanger, and asked me to spend a day at Garonville where the renowned lady had her famous class. It was a village a good distance from Paris, an hour by train. We had lunch with the students in a large studio, and I was fascinated by the many photographs on the walls of a pretty girl in spangles riding a beautiful white horse; the lady in charge of the house had been a bareback rider.

I was too shy to take in the names of the students, who must have become famous in later years. This was in 1926. But I will never forget Mademoiselle Boulanger being shown my first notebook of a few Gaelic songs – saying that they were most unusual and worth collecting. I was envious of Katherine and her friends who after a late session rode their bicycles back to Paris that night, at dawn down the Champs Elysées and round and round the Place de la Concorde with no traffic and the city not yet awake.

It was New Year's Day in Paris, and everyone had gone out to enjoy themselves. My sister Biddy had been taken by a young man from Oxford, a Rhodes scholar, to have fun. I was left to entertain myself, which was not a hardship; but I thought I should give myself some pleasure, so I went out to the Boulevard Montparnasse where, before a wine shop, there were bins of bottles. I bought a bottle of the cheapest champagne. It had to be drunk from a thick jelly glass and the taste was similar to that of Ivory soap. I pretended that it was good, and then thought of a little joke. I put the full laundry bag in Biddy's bed, and my brown fur gloves on the pillow. I had the strange sensation of floating above the bed. I was more than sound asleep when I was wakened to hear a frantic whisper in my ear: 'There's somebody in my bed!' Through my coma I felt a happy satisfaction, and slept again.

There were many White Russians trying to make a living in Paris. Dressmaking was one of their talents and they made pretty clothes at little cost. A charming countess (they always seemed to be countesses) came to the pension for orders and fittings, and she would tell fortunes with cards. My sister Biddy was told of a happy marriage, and so were the other girls. When the countess came to me, she was puzzled and then serious. 'I can see for you a most interesting life, not unhappy, but so different.' This pleased me, though I could see nothing in myself to bring it about. What did make me feel different was my silk dress which she had made with wide bands of rust, orange and cream, an embroidered panel in the front of the skirt and wide sleeves in the same colours. She made me a Russian blouse of rough cotton with a stand-up collar, trimmed in red. I had never had such fine clothes, like nobody else's.

Biddy and I started from Paris on a tour of Ireland, making our way to Cork where we first went to kiss the Blarney Stone. The aperture was in the top of the high tower where you lay flat on your back and grasped the iron rods that were opposite the hole in the wall, and so lowered the head down to kiss the stone. Both of us, being very short, depended on a policeman to hold our ankles. I viewed the tops of tall pine trees below and held so fast to the rods that I took much skin off the backs of my hands. It did nothing for our tongues.

I then wanted to hear the bells of Shandon on the River Lea and we arrived at the door, only to be surrounded by ragged children begging, who were then chased away by the verger shouting, 'Yer a disgrace to the mithers that reared ye.'

Being May, the hedgerows were in bloom – the green fields with shafts of sunlight between the clouds, the massive purple mountains, colours that are only to be found in Ireland. We wandered through Killarney north to Malraney where I had a sight of poverty with the little cabins on the desolate moors. I remember a long talk with a handsome woman who wore several blouses quilted into one to cover the holes.

On the way to Limerick we shared a carriage with a young girl on her way to America. Her father, with his eyes streaming tears, had put her suitcase in the rack and asked us to look after her. She insisted on leaning out the window to wave her last goodbye and had struck her wrist on a passing train which gave her a frightful bruise; it might really have been broken. Her tears, though, were not only for the pain and for leaving home forever, but for fear that she might be turned back.

We were fast running out of money but found that Lucky Strikes (which we doled out from our carton) were far more acceptable to the porters than money. Biddy insisted that a horse cab would be cheaper than a taxi in Dublin and we put it on the hotel bill.

On the Monday I was given a newspaper which told of the murder of Kevin O'Higgins on the Sunday. It was so horrible – shot through his hands that covered his face. The waitress, an elderly lady with her white hair drawn back in a tight bun, had just put my bacon and egg before me as I read. At my showing her the news, she replied that it was a pity to shoot him on his way to Mass but that he *had* reduced the old age pension a shilling! I thought I would never face bacon and eggs again.

We watched the funeral procession, all the senators, W.B. Yeats, Michael Collins' sister and so many distinguished men and women who looked their part. Then within a few days, there was the funeral procession of Madame Markiewicz, the leader of the Irish Republicans and sister of Maud Gonne. The many who followed looked a different type, dark-haired and thin-faced – a strange contrast to the other procession, as though they were of another race.

Next to the hotel in Harcourt Street was a museum of paintings where, it being free to the public, I spent much of my time. It was a splendid collection, mostly of Irish painters. They have now been removed to Leinster House. There were many other places we could have gone, but we were so short of money that we couldn't afford the tram fare. Biddy thought we could economise by going without lunch, so I was always hungry. When it came to settle our bill, we discovered that lunch had been included in the cost of the room! Staying at this private hotel was Mrs Costello; her husband was a physician in Tuam and she was a senator from County Mayo. It was from Mrs Costello that I first heard of collecting Gaelic folksongs, and it was her book, *Amhrain Mhuighe Seola*, that showed me how it should be done. She published all the verses so that the songs were complete; she also included notes on where they were found, who gave them, and references to other songs. What Mrs Costello did was to translate, line for line, putting it down exactly, and that's what gave me my key to writing the music down and getting all the words translated, line for line. The words are the most important thing for the singers; the tune is just the carriage that carries the words. I learned that right away at Mairi MacRae's; no matter how cracked or awful the voice was in singing, the words had to be absolutely pure, so that everybody listening got the poetry. And I thought then how vastly important this is to singers to know that the words must be heard, that they should love the poetry.

I found some Belgian francs of Biddy's and took them down to Thomas Cook's, changed them and got just enough money to buy this book – 7/6d. Biddy, when she found out, cried, 'You're nothing but a common thief!' But I got what I wanted.

CHAPTER FOUR

South Uist

I HAD HOPED to be a pianist, but I developed rheumatism, really some kind of an infection which affected my joints, making them terribly sore so that I couldn't play. I had my appendix out and my tonsils and wisdom teeth, and underwent all kinds of treatment to find a cure. Aunt Elsie, who was generous and loving, and lovely to look at, paid all my expenses for all this time; I think I saw twenty-three doctors. The doctor I saw in New York was a specialist, Dr Russell Cecil. He said to me, when I was getting better, 'Margaret, you have too many relations! What would you like to do?' And I said, 'Well, I've been on a bicycle tour through the Hebrides, and I would like to go back there, to live and to collect songs and learn Gaelic.' And he said, 'Why, that's a wonderful idea! My wife is Australian, but her ancestors came from the Hebrides, and it's a place I've always wanted to visit. That's what you should do.'

So I went back to Glenshaw and announced that I was going to go to South Uist. And they all had a fit! They thought that riding the bicycle – using the handbrakes – was perhaps the cause of the trouble, and getting wet and that I hadn't looked after myself.

When Aunt Mary asked what I planned to do in South Uist, I said I wanted to collect folksongs. In trying to explain, I mentioned that Percy Grainger had done that in Ulster, and she said, 'But *he's* a musician!' And Uncle George said, 'You know, we had a distant cousin called Dude Weighly; her name was Dorothy, but she was called Dude. She eventually lived with the cats and the chickens and became very peculiar. Now you don't want to be another Dude Weighly, surely?' And they thought I was ungrateful, and that I would never amount to anything, and it was a waste of a life, and so on. It was all very sad and difficult. However, something made me go. So I started off to South Uist.

Of all the islands I'd visited, there was something about South Uist that just won me; it was like falling in love; it was the island that I wanted to go back to. Of course, I was not looking for *islands*: I was looking for a way to live my life. I went first to Lochboisdale and stayed in a cottage with a Mrs Campbell for two or three months, but there was too much English, and it wasn't exactly what I wanted. Donald Ferguson, who was a cousin of Mrs Campbell's, asked us to Boisdale House for New Year's dinner. So we went around to South Lochboisdale, where we had a lovely dinner, and afterwards Mrs Campbell said, 'What about Peigi and Mairi giving us a song?' They came in from the kitchen, and Mairi sang a song which was absolutely wonderful to me; I'd never heard anything like it, and I said, 'Would you teach me that song?' And she said, 'Yes! If you'll come and see me, I'll teach you that song.' 'Right, I'll come!'

A week later I was able to get a boat over the loch, to the south side where they lived. I walked up to this little thatched house with a blue door and I thought, 'This is where I ought to stay, this is where I want to be, if she'll take me.' So I said to her, 'Could I come here and stay? Would you take me as a boarder?' And she said, 'Yes, if you'll be comfortable here, of course I'll take you.' And that was the beginning. I said, 'Well, I have to go home to my sister's wedding, but I'll be back in about six weeks.' And so I went home to my sister Biddy's wedding, and I came back and moved in with Mairi MacRae, and I lived there for four winters and six summers.

Donald Ferguson had a large farm in South Lochboisdale and his big house also included the shop and post office. The two sisters, Peigi and Mairi, were his cousins, their mothers being sisters. In

Boisdale House they were the servants: Mairi the laundry maid and Peigi was both cook and dairymaid and ruled over all. She had a young lass to help her, for the work was never-ending; they were up at five in the morning and never ceased until midnight. The farm-hands were to be fed as well as their other cousin, Angus MacCuish, who was in charge of the shop.

I would come to the kitchen in the late evenings when they would all be having tea and there would always be songs. Peigi and Angus gave me one in praise of Uist with a fine tune and splendid verses:

> O my country, I think of thee, fragrant fresh Uist.
> Land of bent grass, land of barley,
> Land where everything is plentiful,
> Where young men sing songs and drink ale.

Then follows the verse:

> They come to us, deceitful and cunning,
> In order to entice us from our homes;
> They praise Manitoba to us,
> A cold country without coal or peat.
> I need not trouble to tell you it;
> When one arrives there one can see – a short summer, a
>   peaceful autumn
> And long winter of bad weather.

This song reminded me of a woman I met on the roadside who said that since I came from America I might know her son who had gone to Saskatchewan: 'The frost is in their bones and they miss the sea.'

My coming to live with Mairi and her son Donald meant that she no longer needed to work in the laundry. She now had a little money to be independent. It was the same for Peigi when she was old enough to receive the pension and came to live at home with Mairi.

They had both been on the mainland where they learnt English when young. Mairi had been with an elderly spinster near Glasgow who had been kind and patient, teaching her by giving a list of things she must take to the grocer, repeating the names of each item. Peigi had had a much harder time. She was sent as a servant to Donald Ferguson's sisters in Edinburgh. Their house was in a row of tall houses, all with white steps. Peigi knew the way home and which house it was – they were difficult to tell apart for her – because in the window there was a white china swan with a plant in it. The cousins sent her to the Pentland Hills, outside Edinburgh, a long way off, with a bucket; there were sheep on those hills, and they wanted the manure for their garden. So they sent her off, and she got lost. She wandered all over the hills, but she got her bucket of sheep dung and started back. It was by then gloaming, and they pulled the curtains which meant that she couldn't see the swan! She was wandering around the streets and met a policeman who recognised her because he was courting the maid in the next house. So he said, 'Where are you going and what's that you've got in your bucket?' She showed him the sheep dung and said that she'd been out on the hills, and he said, 'This is a very dangerous thing to do at night, to go out in the evening like that!' He began telling her that she should never do such a thing and so on. And she finally said in her broken English, 'I can't find my door!' And so he took her home to the house, and the sisters, who were older than she, thought that this was a big joke – very funny. She was there two or three years before going back to Lochboisdale.

Peigi used to go to what they called the 'gutting', as a member of a crew – five girls who went together to herring stations, ports on the east coast of Scotland. There were huge troughs, where the girls would gut the herring and salt and pack them in barrels. Peigi was a wonderful sailor, never seasick, never afraid of the sea, whereas the 'gutter girls' as we called them, were always terrified of the sea and were violently seasick. She told me about going from Lochboisdale down to Oban on a dreadful day. The girls were very frightened –

lying on the deck, practically passing out with sea-sickness, and she was singing! She was a wonderful singer; she never stopped singing on land or sea. She sang all the time, and the fishermen were so delighted with her that they tied her to a chair and tied the chair to the mast so that she could sing all the way to please them. And the girls were shouting and crying and bawling, 'you'll take us right to Hell with your songs! . . . We should be praying God to save us', and so on. This she thought was very funny.

Peigi was a tiny wee thing; I felt just huge beside her – and I'm five feet one. Peigi and Mairi had the greatest wisdom, tolerance, cheer, and courage, and yet had so little. They were glad to have nice things, but they didn't expect them. They had enough food, and they took great pleasure in what they did possess. They had no envy. That was their way of life; they were accustomed to it. And of course it was much better in the years I was there than it had been in years before.

When people in Glenshaw saw the film I had made in South Uist, they were amazed that everybody seemed to be happy in what appeared to be poverty, that they were laughing. When I went back to Glenshaw in the days of deep Depression, I was horrified to find that people came to the carriage-house where bags of flour were stored for them. When you went to church, you took a jar of jam or whatever could be spared to be distributed to people who'd once been very well off but who were now destitute; they were hungry and had to be fed. They were lost, with no idea of how to cope. And they felt a terrible mortification.

The schoolteacher came to stay with us, Katie Anne Nicolson from Skye. She was a young and jolly girl, just out of teacher's training college. There was to be a *Mod*, a competition on the island, and Katie was persuaded to go, for she had a lovely voice. So we sat on a hill and taught her a song that would be new to the audience. It was really a man's song, but with her full, deep, lovely voice she won the prize. It pleased me to think that I was the one who had given her the song.

Peigi and Mairi's house was a very small cottage. You entered a little passageway, and on your left was what they called 'the room'; and on your right was the kitchen, and then between there was a door to a tiny room which they called 'the closet', *closaid*, where there were two small beds. Mairi's son Donald slept on the bench in the kitchen, and I was given 'the room'. I had my books there, and the spinning-wheel. I had a couch and two upright chairs. When the women came to spin and talk to me, we sat 'up' in my room; when the men came, we sat 'down' in the kitchen.

I had to learn that no one was called by their last name. It was *Peigi Anndra*, meaning Peggy daughter of Andrew, or '*Mairi Mhor an at-Soighdeir*', Big Mary, daughter of the soldier'. If I said that I'd met 'Mary Campbell', Mairi Anndra would say, 'Which one? Do I know her?' I should have said '*Mairi Iain Chlachair*.'

Every night friends would come in to sing and talk. Angus John Campbell was the one who came regularly all the years I was there, and he taught me an enormous amount, in knowledge of songs as well as the Gaelic words for birds and the parts of a boat. These latter were often of Norse derivation from the Viking inheritance. I can see him yet, after a long evening of instruction, taking a live peat from the fire in the tongs and going out in the pitch-black. The wind would make the peat flare up like a torch to light his way home. The path was between deep ditches – peat bogs in which one could drown. A huge Highland bull was found up to his head and there was a struggle to put a rope round his horns, with all the men pulling to save the beast from sure death.

And the storms! The thatch was rounded, and the ends of the houses were rounded, so there was nothing to catch the wind. Everything just blew across it, unless the wind came from the north-east, with rain; then that was hard on the door, and I've seen water hit the door and then just rise up like a little curtain underneath with such force of the wind. The storms used to be so bad in the winter that all the peat, the whole fire, would blow right into the middle of the floor from the chimney. I'd rush, and grab peat and a shovel, and put it back and pound it out.

We always had cats, a dog, and a very good Highland cow for milk, and pet lambs: they made pets of everything, including the ram. Once when Mairi had a headache and was in the *closaid* lying in bed, I was at the kitchen table, about to clean a little cockerel we were to eat. Mairi called to me to 'take the engine out'. So I started with great difficulty and, as I began to get the inside out, I suddenly looked sideways, and in the door came the ram, a huge thing with great curly horns. He was coming right for me because he wanted to get to a bin of potatoes that was under the chest. I didn't want him to get in, so I picked up a saucepan that was lying on the table, and as I did this, the chicken began to move: the cat was pulling the chicken in my left hand and I had the saucepan with my right, trying to hit the ram. Mairi heard this shouting and swearing and put her head around the door. It cured her headache, she said, to see me. The ram and Fluffy the cat had me at a great disadvantage.

Willy-cat was found as a kitten in the shop on the pier at Lochboisdale. Mr Clark had a shop in which he sold everything from cheese to corsets, and he always had a lot of cats. These kittens were running all over the food and everything, and the boy that worked for him said, 'Mairi, take a kitten, take a kitten!' So she picked up this cute little brown furry kitten and stuck it in her jacket and took it home. That one became Wicked Willy. He was a remarkable cat. When Fluffy had kittens, Willy would bring her mice to her basket. He was the most devoted tom, very sweet, and when I was married, Mairi said, 'You must take Willy with you'. So Willy then went to live on Barra, and then later we brought him to Canna.

They had their own peat-bank just down from the croft, below the house. Everybody had their own peat bog; a certain part belonged to each family. There were about thirteen families in that whole glen, and the men would help each other. The neighbours, with Donald, would cut Mairi's peat one day, and then Donald would go with them to cut Angus Ruadh's peat, and each house that was having peat cut would give them a good meal and would always give them a twist of tobacco and a half-crown if they could afford it. You cut the peat in June, but you wanted good weather for it. You cut it just like chocolate cake, in pieces, and then you took it onto the bank and you put three or four together to dry, and then you added more and more, and then when it was properly dried, you took it home and made the big peat-stack. They had a way of making it so that it shed the water; the ones on top were left wet, but it was always dry underneath. The blacker the peat, the better, for it dries as hard as iron and burns far longer. They would cut enough to last a year. They would never let a peat fire go out but smother it with ash at night and blow it into life in the morning.

In the spring, Mairi and Donald would mark the long strips on their land for what they called 'lazy-bed', and cover each strip with seaweed. Then between each strip they would dig out the sods and lay them on the seaweed. This made a ditch on each side that drained the water. They then made holes in the sods with a dibble called a *pleadhag*, and planted potatoes. These were delicious and the mainstay of our diet.

The seaweed was also spread on the field and the earth was turned over with a foot-plough, called a *cascrom*, meaning 'crooked foot'. The lumps of earth were broken up with a heavy wood rake with five thick teeth, and then a harrow was dragged by hand to smooth the ground and the oats were sown.

The few sheep were carefully tended, the male lambs sold for the money needed to buy tea, sugar and other necessities, the ewe lambs kept to replenish the herd. They would never eat their own sheep, but the local mutton was the best ever tasted. They were a small breed of 'Blackface' and fed on the salty grass, heather and seaweed so the mutton was never fat and greasy.

They grew potatoes and oats and that's all. They couldn't grow cabbages or anything like that because the sheep could get into everything; fences were expensive, and it was just not done. So we never had any green vegetables, and I was never so well in my life.

I was worried about them when I saw that they didn't have medical attention and proper food. Now, I thought to myself, I can't live without oranges and prunes, and I couldn't afford them, because I'd have had to share them with innumerable children around who'd never seen an orange! But I found that on porridge and herring I could manage very well, and I got my vitamins in marmalade. I never missed the other things. Of course I was fortunate that I could go over to the hotel on Sunday for dinner.

I remember remarking to the minister, 'What I see is that only people with running water in their houses can take Communion.'

'Margaret!'

'Well,' I said, 'look around. There is a church filled – the excise-man and his wife, the doctor and his wife, the hotel owner and others well off, but nobody else. Look at Peigi and Mairi Anndra. Where are they?'

'They would be too shy to come to the Lord's Table.'

'But you've never asked them.'

He knew quite well what I meant, and in fact he agreed with me.

We were so glad to get a bird, because meat was very scarce and extremely expensive. And we were far away from shops and places where you could get good things. Angus John once brought me a *guilbneach* – a curlew. The curlew is a biggish bird on the shore or on the moors. It has a lovely call and a curved beak which turns down. They are so hard to shoot that it is said that there are only twelve curlews in the life of a man. We cooked Angus' curlew in the iron pan on top of the fire, and it was the best thing I ever ate. Mairi said, 'We'll leave the juice in the pan now and keep that. It won't go bad; we'll just keep that.' When we later had the chicken I'd prepared, we cooked it in the juice of the curlew, and the chicken was almost as good as the curlew. We also cooked shags. I remember with the first one, I thought I ought to pluck it. I tried, and it was like plucking a carpet. It was terrible to get it off, and then the skin was awfully black and funny. Then I was told you must never do that: you skin it, take the whole skin off. And then you soak the bird in a sort of salty water, and dry it, and then cook it, and it's quite good. Otherwise, it's terribly fishy. I never ate a heron. Angus John said that you could eat a heron, but you'd have to catch it when it's a full moon, otherwise it's nothing but bones and skin; at the full moon, though, they're fishing all night, and then they get fat.

We got things from the sea, of course. The men who fished for lobsters to send away would give us one now and then, and we had mackerel and other fish. We used to take a big round net, just like a sieve with a handle. We would go out in the boat, and we would put down the circular net, the *tamh*, scattering bread or bits of shellfish like limpets, and these little *cudaigean* would come in their hundreds when we dipped the net. They were just delicious fried. You could eat the whole thing, bones and all. They all ate salt herring; this was the great thing! But it was so salty I couldn't eat it. I can see yet the iron pot, the only pot we used for it, which was all rusty, and when it boiled, all the stuff on the top, all the scum, bubbles, everything was all brown and horrible. But they adored it. They poured it through a sieve and ate it with their fingers, very delicately.

I'll never forget once when I *had* to eat herring. I had a parcel to take to the minister who was rather an eligible bachelor. He had a housekeeper who didn't like to have anybody come near the door who might catch him, because she had her hopes for him herself. I had a long, long walk there, and when I finally arrived, she opened the door but then shut it in my face. She called Mr MacLeod. He appeared and said, 'Won't you come in? I'm just about to have my lunch, so have lunch with me.' We had salt herring, which was the saltiest thing ever and filled with millions of bones, and before I really got started she took the plate away from me, and then she produced a pudding. The pudding was sago; it was absolute glue, though it looked very nice on the top. He put in the spoon; the whole thing went up with the spoon and then snapped right back again! He could not get any loose on the plate at all. And I can still see him, trying to take a spoon of that pudding, which went way up and then thunk! back down to the dish.

They didn't soak the salt herring at any time, they just washed it and put it in this pot. I think that was one of the reasons that so many people got stomach ulcers; I'm sure it was from eating so much salt. During the war, when Peigi was staying with me here on Canna, we got a big basket of herring, and, because we couldn't possibly eat them all, she said, 'Now, we must salt these; we must save them.' I had no bowl big enough, so we put them in the china umbrella stand. We packed them with plenty of coarse salt, right up to the top, and then I put on the bread board for a lid. Peigi ate them with great pleasure.

Peigi made *maragan*; that's from the intestines of sheep. She would take the liver and lungs and would chop it all with oatmeal and the blood; she would soak the intestines and turn them inside out to be the casing. When it has the blood in it, it's black pudding; with white pudding, it's oatmeal. They don't put anything in that might not keep. Sometimes they put a little onion in it, if they're going to eat it pretty soon. Black pudding is terribly good, but you don't want to watch it being made otherwise you'd never eat it again.

The MacRae cottage had a thatched roof. The yellow weed that grew up there was ragwort, called 'Stinking Willie', after the Duke of Cumberland – Bloody Cumberland of Culloden. The story is that the seeds for this plant, which now grows all over Scotland, came in the feed for Cumberland's horses. As with other plants, ragwort was encouraged since it was used in making dyes. The MacRae cottage had been originally what is called a 'black house'. A black house had no chimney; the fire was on the floor in the centre, and there was a hole in the roof for the smoke to escape. The fire of course was a peat fire; the smoke would gather in the rafters, making a tarry substance, which would drip from them. As the song in praise of the maiden who had a stocking on her knitting needles says, 'She knits while the sooty ooze drops from the rafters'. By my time most of the houses in South Uist had chimneys and were thatched. The old 'black houses', *taighean dubha*, were fast disappearing. I made a count for Eriskay and South Uist in 1933 and found there were thirty-three black houses still inhabited.

Sir Ian Colquhoun of Luss had written to ask me if I could make this. When he later came to South Uist, he asked where I was. One day when he came to the hotel, it so happened I was there because it was the only chance I had of washing my hair. I was told there was somebody to see me and I appeared at the top of the stairs and looked over to see Rex Benson in his deerstalker hat, very haughty. 'Are you Miss Shaw? Sir Ian Colquhoun to see you.' And from behind him walked this man in a very old kilt and a bandanna tied around his neck, but most distinguished looking, like a royalist of the seventeenth century. And he gave me a low bow and came with his hand outstretched and said: 'I want to thank you for your list. It has helped me so much because we hope to make one of these houses into a museum.' And so it was.

I was once asked by the Exciseman to go with him to one such house to interpret, as he knew no Gaelic. The old woman who lived there knew no English; she was claiming the old age pension and he had to determine her age. She lived in a black house built of sods. I'd never been inside one before. When we came to it and knocked, hens flew out from holes in the thatch; the dogs' noses were under the door. The old woman opened the door a crack and called off the snarling dogs, and then she realised who we were and led us back in to a pitch-black room. When I began to see, I could make out that there were boards across to make a partition, beyond which they obviously kept animals. 'Ask how old she is,' he said to me, but I didn't know how to say that in Gaelic but I could say, '*C'uine thainig sibh a's an t-saoghal*?' meaning, 'When did you come into the world?' And she turned around and said in Gaelic, 'Ask the priest!' Anybody could tell by looking at her that there was no necessity of going further, that she *did* deserve the pension.

When I returned to the MacRaes' house that evening, I told my story. Such poverty! And why such a miserable house? The reply was, 'There's plenty under the floor!' Everyone had been given a government grant to improve his or her house; she had taken the money and done nothing.

In the course of time the MacRaes were able to build a chimney at each end of the house and line the ceiling and the walls. The peat fire smoke had stained the paper, so Mairi and I re-papered the kitchen; as the ceiling was concave, it was like papering the inside of an elephant! The design was one of rambler roses, very pretty; we felt the kitchen to be like a bower.

Like all the other thatched houses, this one had double walls four feet thick, built of large stones with the space between the two packed with small stones and earth. The windows were set far back to give a deep ledge and here the hens would shelter, blocking out all the light so that I would think it was still night and never get up. Such walls are far better for fending off the cold and storms than the single walls of the modern houses that have replaced many of them. The MacRae cottage was always snug and warm inside, no matter the weather.

The only drawback was that, in winter, harbour rats came in behind the wallpaper to eat the paste. One evening when Johnny Campbell the bard, Angus John Campbell, and Mairi and Donald were helping me to take down their Gaelic songs, Donald, hearing the rats in the wall, began stabbing with his knife, and I said 'Stab through the roses so the knife holes won't show.' But old Johnny said, 'If you don't kill the rat outright, it will come back and do a lot of damage.' He then told us of a fishing boat at the pier, where one of the fishermen threw a stone at a rat without killing it. The others told him he would pay for it. The next morning they found holes gnawed in this man's nets, which were gathered together with the nets of the others in the hold; there were no holes in the nets of the others.

I went off to Lochboisdale the next day, where I was kept by a storm for the night. I came back next morning to find my nutria coat hanging on the back of the door with one huge hole in the seat and another in the side. Mairi greeted me with 'The rats ate it.' 'Mairi, this is my only winter coat, my twenty-first birthday present; I'll never have another.' Mairi's attempt to console me was to say, 'They'll be making nests for the wee ones.' She then showed me Donald's bed where they had eaten a huge hole right through the blankets.

These big, brown Norwegian rats lived on the shore. I've seen them walking under water as if they were on land. They were plentiful in Uist; in fact they had a saying that the day would come when Uist would be given over entirely to the rats. Even Boisdale House suffered rats. Peigi told me how she would make Donald Ferguson a little gruel of wheaten flour and milk, heat it on the stove, and take it up to him in bed. Now he had a little short beard – thick, heavy, white – and one morning he woke up feeling very sore around the mouth; the rats had been finishing off the gruel which was stuck to his whiskers.

It was a near two miles by path from the MacRaes' cottage to the road, and then there was the long seven miles to Lochboisdale. I walked it many a time, stopping at Boisdale House where Peigi would give me a glass of milk or a cup of tea. But the easiest way was to cross the loch by boat. Angus John was the ferryman with his sailing boat, *Gill Brighde*. We would go out the south side of the loch, tacking across to the north and into Lochboisdale pier. The

The author's mother, Fanny Maria
Patchin, aged 18

The author's father as a Civil Engineer
visiting Colón, Panama

Glenshaw, the house of Thomas Wilson Shaw, Glenshaw Valley

RIGHT. Mrs Robert Watson, the author's Great Aunt Ellen, Glenshaw, 1912

BELOW LEFT. The author's father, Henry Clay Shaw (left) and his younger brother Charles as students

BELOW RIGHT. The author (left) and sister, Biddy, with Caesar the cat

Standing Stones at Callernish, Lewis

Standing Stones at Garynahine, Lewis, 1926

House of Broch at Dun Carloway, Lewis

Skye croft and peat stack, Kilmuir, 1924

Thatched house on the Staffin road, Skye, 1927

St Kildans coming out to meet *The Hebrides* on her first call in May 1930

Village Bay, St Kilda, looking across the Church and Manse to the point of Dun, May 1930

Flax wheel spinner, Inishma'an, Aran, Co. Galway

The curragh going ashore at Inishma'an, Aran Islands, Co. Galway, 1930

Children on
Inishma'an, Aran
Islands, Co. Galway

Inishma'an village, Aran Islands, Co. Galway

Carrying turf, Inishma'an, Aran Islands, Co. Galway

Màiri MacRae with Finlay and Queen (right), North Glendale, South Uist, 1930

Màiri MacRae's house, *Tigh Màiri Anndra*, where the author lived in North Glendale

Iain Campbell, mason (*Iain Clachair*), plaiting heather into rope to secure thatch, South Glendale, South Uist. Brother of the bard Johnny Campbell (*Seonaidh Caimbeul*), he was a fine singer as well as composer of songs

Mrs Angus Campbell, *Bean Aonghuis Ruaidh*, raking straw, North Glendale

Mary MacLeod carding wool before spinning

Mary MacLeod at her spinning wheel. A wooden *crois-iarna* for winding and measuring wool hangs on the wall

Màiri MacRae with *Uilleam Dona* ('Wicked Willie') at the fireside, North Glendale, South Uist, 1931

Cutting peats, North Glendale

Peigi MacRae washing clothes at the burn

ABOVE. Peigi MacRae milking Dora, North Glendale, South Uist, 1933

LEFT. Children dressed as guisers for Hallowe'en, South Uist. *Aodannain* (false faces) were made of oilskin or sheepskin, and the child on the right had an entire sheep's head cleaned out and slipped over his head like a bag

ABOVE. *Seonaidh Caimbeul*, the bard, using his *cas chrom*, South Lochboisdale, 1932. His songs were published in 1936

RIGHT. Digging lugworm for flounder bait on the strand at South Glendale, looking to Barra across the Sound of Eriskay

Guillemots on Mingulay, 1933

The lighthouse dinghy, Mingulay, 1932

Kittiwakes and razorbills, Mingulay, 1932

The former Schoolhouse, Mingulay

South Uist in May; resting while herding cattle

Horsefair at Geirnish, South Uist

LEFT. Mrs Mary Campbell (*Bean Iain Chlachair*) with her Hebridean Blackface sheep, South Glendale, South Uist

BELOW. Svolvær, Lofoten Islands, 1935, where the Campbells went for their honeymoon

Tigh Ceann a' Bhaigh, Northbay, Barra, 1936. The 'Gille Brighde' and John Lorne Campbell in the dinghy

Wicked Willie and Mr Smith at the kitchen door, Northbay, Barra

ABOVE. Castlebay and
Kismul Castle, Barra, 1933

RIGHT. Donald MacLeod,
gardener, Canna House,
1942

Canna House

Canna House looking to Sanday

Viking grave, Langanes, Canna

John Lorne Campbell and Pooni, 1949

Canna Harbour, 1955

Three sections of the stone found at Keill, Canna

The author at her typewriter, Canna House

loch was full of islands and one had to thread among the rocks, very dangerous in the dark. During daylight, with the tide high and the load light, we would take a tiny skiff which was able to make the short journey through the narrow passage called 'Crow's Pass'. The skiff was always referred to as 'Callendar', having once belonged to a man of that name.

The *Gille Brighde* was strongly built and gave us assurance in the roughest weather. Angus John was really a part of his beloved boat. He sailed her in difficult waters with the greatest skill. One day Finlay MacKenzie, the proprietor of the Lochboisdale Hotel, suggested to Angus John that he might put an engine in her so that he could take visiting fishermen from the hotel out into the open sea to fish. Finlay said he would pay for the engine, a generous gift that would save Angus John much money. Angus John told me this as we tacked our way across to Lochboisdale. 'There's no exultation in a motor,' he said. 'A wee bit of sail and I can take her out of hell.'

My knowledge of small boats was limited to canoes or dinghies, but I knew that it was important to sit in the middle and never let her be broadside onto the waves. Angus John's rule was never to tie the sheet, to keep it in a strong hand to let out or bring in the sail with the wind's command. The *Gille Brighde* was a heavy boat, seventeen feet long with a draught of three feet and a strong mast. She was steered with a rear tiller, or *stiuir* as he called it. The lug sail was thick canvas dyed a dark brown, which was the colour of all sails in the Islands. The two oars were long and very heavy, but once in place, and with a board to brace one's feet, they were easy to row. I could only manage one because of the weight, but with Angus John or his brother also rowing, I got into the rhythm – and with strength. I know this was because of my years of playing the piano, for I was taught to bring tone with weight from my shoulders. When there was a sign of wind, the sail would be hauled up. Angus John, with the tiller under his left arm and the sheet in his right hand, his pipe filled with finely pared Bogey Roll, the tin lid fastened tight to keep the wind from blowing away his well lit, tightly crammed tobacco, would sail across to Lochboisdale.

I remember one crossing; it was the twenty-third of January, and there was a south-easterly gale with sleet and snow. When the showers came, very fast and hard, it stung your face, and the wind was terribly strong. Angus John, his brother James, and I started back to Glendale. We had to get into the boat at Lochboisdale Pier, hoist the sail for quite a way, then lower the sail and tack in order to enter a channel to reach the other side. It was quite a distance, and very dangerous, of course – pitch black, except when the clouds would lift and some light would come. I had on a big leather coat, and I got down in the bottom of the boat. They put up the sail, and I could see the sail rippling, and then we seemed to stall. I heard Angus John shout to his brother to get the sail down, to get around. We'd got the rope of a lobster creel around the rudder; it could easily have capsized us. Young James had a terrible job in letting the sail down. He was nearly carried over with it – and I could hear Angus John saying in the midst of it in his Gaelic, 'Take her cool, take her cool!' Angus John was running in his white sea-boots; he would run along the gunwale to grab and help get the sail down, and then, when he'd got it down, he put his heels to catch the stern thwart and then leant right over the stern, head and shoulders into the icy water. He took hold of the heavy helm, pulled it out, untangled the rope, and put it back in place again. It was a terrific feat of strength. They took the oars again and rowed into the shelter of an island to get a breath and pull themselves together. Then they rowed out again and we put up a tiny little sail in order to get through the narrows.

And my poor Mairi! She thought we ought to have been home earlier and she was so frightened with the storm that she had come down to the shore with a lantern, but she couldn't see anything nor hear anything for the storm. Crouched in the boat bottom, I thought, 'Well, I'd better take my coat off, because I won't be able to swim with this heavy thing on.' So I slid out of it, whereupon a big wave came over and soaked me to the skin, and I thought, 'No, I'm going to die with my coat on!' So I put it back on to keep warm.

When we at last got over to the shore – home – Mairi was so pleased to suddenly hear our voices! And I crawled out onto the rocks and got up, and I'd been so long curled up into a ball, that I fell right over backwards into a great big puddle! And that made us all roar and laugh.

A man named O'Henley had put the creel in the fairway, which he should never have done. Two nights later, Johnny Campbell's Peigi was not well, and Mairi and I were down there to sit through the night with her. And at about two in the morning, in came Angus John with a great big lobster. 'Here's something I pinched for you – from Angus O'Henley's creel! That's what he's paid for that bad night he gave us!'

The shop at Lochboisdale was kept by Mr F. T. Gillies. I heard from him valuable accounts from the history of the Hebrides. The sitting room above his shop was where I would spend evenings listening to this learned and kindly man tell of the old days, especially of the evictions when the people were cleared from their land to give it to sheep farmers from the south of Scotland. The people were forced to leave and told that Canada was where they would find a far better life. A ship called at Lochboisdale to take them away. Some men were tied with ropes and put aboard, others hid in the hills.

Mr Gillies' father was a blacksmith in North Uist, known as a man of tremendous strength and independent character, opposing the Church of Scotland which was subsidised by the government and which approved of the evictions. One day the people of his village were all told to come to the church to a meeting. While they were there, the sheriff and his officers began clearing their cottages of contents and burning the thatched roofs. When the smith realised what was happening, he rushed back to find his wife had been carried out with her new-born baby and the furniture was just being removed by the sheriff's men. He shouted to put it all back or he would break every bone in their bodies. Their fear of this powerful man made them do what they were told, and his house was saved.

I used sometimes to cross to Lochboisdale pier in the *St Bride*, buy my groceries at the shop, and then walk the nine miles home with them. I used to walk a lot in those days; I loved it. Once I was carrying home a big, badly tied parcel of groceries. It was a misty evening; fog was rolling in from the Atlantic. I had on a black oilskin and a black sou'wester. The road was very lonely; there were no more than four or five cars on the island at the time. To get home I had to pass a hill, a low hill covered with rocks and grass, called Carishaval, which was said to be haunted. There were said to be ghosts there.

Well, just there the string of my big parcel broke. I got down on the roadside in the grass to try to tie it up again. A long way off – Uist is bare, without trees – I could see a cyclist coming along the road, but he didn't see me. I rose up at the side of the road and said '*Oidhche mhath*!' 'Good evening!' The bicycle went swerving every which way down the road; I had given him the most terrible fright. I'm sure he swears he heard a *bocan* on Carishaval!

Once, on an afternoon in Christmas week, I walked to Daliburgh at the head of Lochboisdale, to a friend's cottage. I had with me Mr Gillies' collie, a very young dog. I got there and had tea; then I thought I'd walk up to the machair and then get back on the road, making a sort of circle to Lochboisdale. I got out to the machair, which is a great, broad, sandy, grassy plain just at the edge of the Atlantic, where the waves were roaring. But a thick fog suddenly came in, and I couldn't find the road. I couldn't find anything; all I could do was to keep on walking. And of course in the winter the daylight only lasts a very short time, and it began to get dark and the moon came up. The little dog Pat and I had to just keep walking north, always keeping the roar of this surf steady in our left ear, because to the East, where we wanted to go, there were bogs and deep drains where you could drown. I knew I had to keep on walking towards Askernish, a place about three miles farther to the north; I thought I might see a light in some house there which would show me the way to the road.

Now the moon was shining; I could see it above my head, with this thick fog pouring in, and suddenly, swish, there were wings right in my face: we had walked into a great flock of wild geese. They didn't hear us coming, and there they were suddenly, beating their wings as they roared up. We eventually got to Askernish, a long way up the machair, and I realised from a certain light that I was just past the deep drains, and that I should find a wooden bridge – just planks across. We got through there, and then we had the long walk home. I remember Pat running ahead of me in the moonlight, which was then brighter with the fog not so thick. He would run ahead and then lie down flat, absolutely exhausted on the road until I caught up with him, and then he'd get up and start off again, and so on. Instead of coming home at five or six o'clock, I didn't arrive 'till after midnight, and I found that my feet were getting very, very sore. My woollen socks, which of course had got soaked, had completely disintegrated. I hardly had any socks left when I took my shoes off.

I saw at that time, coming back to Lochboisdale, a very strange phenomenon. The mist was still coming in big fragments, flowing in from the west; the moon was shining, and I saw, on the side of a white house that was well in from the road, my shadow, which was absolutely tremendous. I couldn't believe my eyes when I saw this huge creature going along, and then I realised it was myself with the moon and the reflection.

The schoolhouse was more than a mile from Mairi Anndra's and she was in charge of cleaning and putting on the great fire to heat the one room. Early in the morning before the light of day, she would go to have the room warm before the 'scholars', as she called them, and the teacher would arrive. Some of the children came from South Glendale, over the hill beside the Sound of Eriskay. They would cross the hill even when there would be ice on the pools and the grass, running in bare feet the two miles and more to the school. When I expressed my horror and wondered how I could find money for shoes, Mairi said *no*: if they came in wet boots to sit in the school all day, they would then catch their death. Far better their bare feet to dry.

There were some twenty children and at Christmas I thought we should have a party in the school. There never had been a party in their lives. So apples, oranges, and candy were ordered from Oban. Then tea scones and cakes to be baked at home. Angus John would bring his 'box' (accordion) and his brother James, the bagpipes. After the feast we danced, then more tea before we all formed a procession to walk home under the stars with James leading the way, playing the pipes. I have a splendid book on Slavic design given to me by those children who contributed to buying it. In beautiful script it is inscribed, 'From the scholars of Glendale school'.

Two of these little children who were so poor and went barefoot to school – one is now captain of an oil-tanker, and the other one's a mate. They earn enormous salaries, but they come home in the summer to their cottages. It's called 'Millionaire's Row', so the man on the boat told me. Three others were killed in the war. But they all did well.

I achieved a reputation for giving first aid. My little box of bandages, salves, and aspirins was often in use. One day a little girl arrived with a badly cut knee for me to clean. First I would wash such wounds with green soap and hot water, then apply the salve and bandage. This child needed a lot of bandages, and I told her to come the next day for a clean dressing. She did not come, partially due to her not understanding English, for all the young children spoke only Gaelic, learning English in school. A few days later, Mairi Anndra told me that my patient was coming up the path. She had seen the child was still wearing the bandage which was filthy and stank. I hurried to boil the kettle, fill a basin, and while she sat on the bench I sat before her on a milking stool and began to remove the bandage. It was cement. When I started the soaking and gentle pulling, Mary Bella fainted, fell over me so we were both on the floor and the bowl of hot and filthy water covered us. Mairi Anndra put Mary Bella back on the bench and I took the opportunity to yank off the bandage. Her mother appeared in the door, not to console her child but to comfort me. The child revived at once, and we decided to leave the wound open to the air and it healed in no time. I found that such wounds generally healed slowly because the children were so undernourished.

Another remedy for deep cuts was Archangel Tar. Johnny Campbell showed me a scar in the palm of his hand, made by a crab shell, which was healed by this tar after other treatments had failed. For toothache, he recommended a mixture of gun-powder and tallow to fill the cavity.

I went to a sale of work at the Catholic church and bought tickets for a prize of a lantern, a live chicken, and a dead duck; everybody bought tickets for all these things. To my mortification, I won the rooster and the dead duck. Fortunately, I had a barn-lantern, a storm-lantern with me, since it was night when I started home with the live rooster and the dead duck. And I remember I nearly fell over a white cow that was lying just in front of me; I never even saw it, with the storm and the wind and rain. I never saw this thing till I nearly fell over it. I weaved my way round, found the little foot-bridge and at last got home.

Now this huge, white rooster had a beautiful big tail, and I called him Jonathan Edwards. I thought it rather funny to give him that name when I'd got him from the Catholic sales. Well, a day or two later, I looked out and here was the poor rooster – his head was down, his tail was down; he looked just about to drop dead, you know, he looked absolutely awful. And I said to Mairi: 'Look at Jonathan Edwards. I think he's going to die; he looks awful.' 'Oh no,' said Mairi, 'We'll fix him.' So Donald brought him in. He took a saucer of water, and added a great tablespoon or more of Epsom salts, and stirred it round. Then he turned the rooster on his back, between his knees – the rooster was so far gone that he hardly knew what was happening and opened his beak. Then Donald took a swig from this saucer and shot it, in a silver flash, right into the beak of the rooster! This was repeated several times. Then he shook the rooster and sat him down. And, before you knew it, the rooster was up and shaking his feathers and went on from there.

Peigi loved a dram of whisky – she was never tight, ever – and she used to say to me: 'Now, never put water in your whisky; it's bad for your stomach, you see. You should drink whisky neat.' Which she always did and certainly never showed any bad effect; she was in excellent health and lived to be ninety-six. When she had 'flu, not long before she died, I went out to see her. I'd heard that she'd said she hadn't been at all well and had been confined to her bed. Now, the blankets on her bed were hand-woven – heavy, hand-spun woollen blankets – and she was so little and frail. So I went over with some cellular blankets. I had two Americans staying with me on Canna, and they went with me, but I made them stay way down the road as I went up by myself, because I was afraid that something might have happened to her; it was two or three days before I could get to Uist. I went in the door, and Mairi was in the kitchen. 'Oh, Peigi's in the room,' and I went up, and she was in bed. 'Oh, Maighread Maighread!' She was so glad to see me. She was always clear-headed anytime, and so I said to Mairi, 'I wonder if she could have a dram, because I have a half-bottle with me.' 'I think it would do her good.' So I got a little wee glass, and I poured a little whisky in, and I put some water in it. I took it up to her room to her, and her nephew lifted her up. She sipped and made a horrible face, 'Ugh!' she said, 'Where's the whisky?' So I threw it out the door and poured in the whisky straight.

They were accustomed to drinking whisky, but when I first went to live with Mairi, I didn't like to bring whisky home; I thought it

wasn't done for women to drink whisky. And so I brought a bottle
of very good sherry. One evening when we had visitors, I got out
the sherry; they had no glasses, but they had cups. There were two
fishermen there, two brothers, neighbours, who had come to the
ceilidh, and so I gave everybody sherry in a cup and a little bowl,
and I gave them a decent amount. Mairi had had earache, a sore
head, and she had her head all tied up in a big woolly scarf. We were
sitting looking into the fire, when I suddenly heard Mairi, *'Tha mi
dall! Tha mi dall!'* ('I'm blind! I'm blind!') And the teacher, who was
sitting on the bench between these two men, began to roar and laugh
and lean over so that she could have fallen down on the earthen
floor, which was very uneven, and these two men were holding her
back by the arms while she was in hysterics, yelling and laughing. I
couldn't imagine what was the matter with them; it never occurred
to me that they were tight! Poor Mairi, shouting, 'I'm blind, I'm
blind!' tried to put her head in a crack between two big meal chests!
I didn't know what to do, but Donald and Angus John said, 'Put
the kettle on, Miss Shaw. Make a strong cup of tea.'

And I poked the fire and tried to get the kettle to boil, while they
carried these two women and stretched them out on their beds, and
then they came down. By this time the kettle was boiling and they
made the tea. They took it up in saucers, black tea. And then they
came down and said, 'Now, they're all right there for the night,
but don't ever bring sherry; you see, they're not accustomed to it.
You're far better to bring whisky, because the sherry doesn't agree
with them well.' And they never told, those two men. Mairi and
the school-teacher could have been the laughing-stock of the whole
of South Uist, but they never told that story about the schoolteacher
in hysterics, and Mairi blind, and myself, terrified.

One time I went up to Grogarry in the north end of South Uist
to spend a few days and stayed at the Post Office with a Miss
MacRury. There was a theology student from Lewis who was
boarding at the farm up the road, and I went to him for lessons

in reading Gaelic. I had my grammar, and we always had *Litir a Bearnaraidh*, the late John N. MacLeod's weekly Gaelic column in *The Stornoway Gazette*, 'A Letter from Bernera', an island off the coast of Lewis. This always had a very good Gaelic story. But with the sentences from my book that I had to translate, I was very slow. I remember the embarrassment when I said, 'The cow called. We will have milk on Tuesday.' Well of course to have a cow 'call' means that she calls for the bull. When I said, 'The cow called', my tutor was very much embarrassed, but he didn't explain to me what 'call' meant; only that what I should say was 'The cow calved'.

I remember teasing him, saying that the Hebridean women worked so hard and they always seemed to be carrying the bundles or the sack on their backs while their husbands walked ahead with a stick, and he said, 'Oh not at all! The Hebridean has the highest respect for his women. What you say isn't true at all.' Well I picked up my book of sentences, which was written by a Lewis man, and read 'John, come in. Mary, get up and give him your chair.' And I said, 'There's my case.'

I made many a mistake with words. One occasion shows how very polite the neighbours were. One who was very poor was suffering toothache and had come up to Mairi Anndra's and was sitting on the bench. I came in and said, 'Would you like to hear my Gaelic? *Cia mar a tha do dheargain?*' Mairi Anndra turned to me and said, '*Deideadh! Deideadh!*' When Peigi Neill had gone, Mairi Anndra looked at me and said, '*Deargain! Agus ise lan dhiu!*' (Fleas! And she full of them!) What I had said was, 'How are your fleas?' With her politeness, she'd never let on that I'd said the wrong word! She knew what I meant to say was 'How is your toothache', and thanked me very much.

They were never curious about my background or where I came from, although they knew I came from America. (I had nothing to connect me with the mainland of Britain.) As far as they were concerned, I was like a strange bird that had flown in from the west; that was the way they took me. They took me for myself.

Mairi Anndra would scold me or correct me if necessary, but I had much warmth from everyone. Peigi and Mairi used to call me 'Maighread'. Anyone else always spoke of me as 'Miss Shaw'; I was always known as 'Miss Shaw'. To this very day, after being married many years to John Campbell, when I meet my friends on the road in Uist, they say 'Miss Shaw! And how is your husband?'

It was a life that I loved. I never looked at it from an anthropological point of view or anything else like that at all. It was just for the pure enjoyment. I loved the songs. The tunes were heavenly. They appreciated the fact that I didn't want the songs that were well known: I wanted their own everyday songs, songs that they sang when they rocked the cradle or worked the spinning wheel. These songs had not been much collected before, and had not been really appreciated by collectors. That gave my friends pleasure, and they were anxious to help.

I had to forget the major and minor scales and listen to modes which I had never notated before. I knew how to do it, but I had to concentrate. I had to learn to listen outside of what I had ever heard before, because, even though I took down the tune as accurately as I possibly could, I couldn't get certain half tones that were in it, and nobody can tell except the singer – and then she couldn't read the music!

I knew that one can't take down a Gaelic song without knowing the words, because the difference between the long and short vowels of the language are so much a part of the rhythm of the tune. So I tried to learn the language, and when I began I knew absolutely nothing. I would get somebody like Angus John Campbell to help me write it down, and, though he didn't know much about writing Gaelic, he knew enough to repre-sent it phonetically. In his writing I could see the stress of syllables, and then in hearing it I could find the syllables that went under the notes of the tune. In Gaelic songs, the tune just carried the words along. If the voice was good, that was very nice, but it wasn't essential. The first thing was to hear the poem.

They were polite when we were gathering in the kitchen; everybody would be asked to sing. There was one neighbour who was a bit feeble-minded, Mary Kate, and she had two songs which she sang to the same tune, but that made no difference. They listened to Angus John singing a very fine song, but she got just the same applause. They made Kate feel just as important as anyone there. And they were very tolerant of me.

I first met Seonaidh Caimbeul (Johnny Campbell) on top of the hill called Gearsinis, behind his house. I was walking over the hill through heather and long grass. At the brink of the hill, his face, like a gnome's, looked up at me. He was lying flat on his tummy on the hill, looking out at something. He had a funny felt hat with the brim turned up in front. He had a little white goatee and the brownest, big bright eyes. When he looked up, I thought, 'Well, you are the most adorable thing I've ever seen!'

He was a delightful man. He and his wife Peigi were neighbours. He was a fine Gaelic poet; his songs were very popular at Uist ceilidhs. He carried them all in his head; I don't think he could write much more than his own name in English, and he certainly never learned to write Gaelic, his native language. It wasn't taught in school at all when he was young. After 1934, his songs were written down from his dictation by a neighbour, John MacInnes OBE, and the total came to about a hundred; a selection of about forty-five was published in a little book called *Orain Ghaidhlig le Seonaidh Caimbeul* – in English, *Gaelic Songs by Johnny Campbell*.

His brother Iain Clachair (which means John the stone-mason) also made poems. Both were called 'John' in English, something that used to happen in large families in Uist in the old days, and distinguished in Gaelic by being called 'Seonaidh' and 'Iain'. Iain built a very fine Catholic church on the Isle of Barra. He used to make his measurements by using a stick with little notches; I don't think *he* ever really learned to read or write either. And yet he built this fine building; he was just born for that.

Johnny Campbell wrote very good poetry – very funny poetry. There were some cows washed ashore from a ship which was sunk and they were buried, but not deep enough so that the other cows smelt the blood and began to paw and snort, and it was a terrible hullaballoo to get the cows away from that site. Seonaidh wrote a poem about that. Another time there was a man who had been mending the schoolhouse roof and had borrowed Seonaidh's ladder, which had been lying outside the school. When Seonaidh appeared over the hill, hoping to collect his ladder, two or three steps were broken; in no time, he'd composed a satire against Neill MacPhee who'd borrowed his ladder. He made a whole poem while he was gathering up his things, which he then recited to Mairi Anndra, who had a great laugh.

Iain and Seonaidh knew much of the classic eighteenth century Gaelic poetry of the Highlands and Islands, poems and songs by bards like Alexander MacDonald, Duncan Ban MacIntyre, John MacCodrum and others, poetry which is beautiful but also very difficult. They knew it by heart and had learnt it by ear and could recite it at great length: poems like Alexander MacDonald's 'Birlinn of Clanranald' and Duncan MacIntyre's 'Praise of Beinn Dorain', a famous mountain in Argyllshire. I had heard parts of this one sung. Mairi said, 'But Iain Clachair knows that, and Seonaidh has it all.' I said 'Seonaidh, will you recite it for me?' Whereupon his nephew Angus John Campbell said, 'Nooooh! It has five hundred lines!'

Seonaidh didn't recite it all, but he gave a tremendous amount of it. He was so enraptured with the actual words and with speaking it, that he was carried away. Afterwards I said to him, 'How did you learn that? Where did you learn it?' 'I learned it like this,' he said, burying his face in his hands. Seonaidh had gone as a young boy to work as a herdsman on the big MacGillivray farm at the north end of the Isle of Barra. There were two men working on the farm who came from the poet's country and they had taught

83

him. This is how all Gaelic poetry was passed down, orally, and those who knew it could spot a wrong word in a single line. Could you find people who had never been taught to read or write English but could recite Milton or Spencer? There were no people like the old tradition-bearers of the Hebrides, and there will be no more like them.

My first thought was to get the songs down and I didn't look beyond that. But when I began looking over what I had, I saw that it was a tapestry: their whole way of life was in the songs. When I did, I decided to make a book of the songs and to put in what I'd absorbed and enjoyed along the way. There would also be photographs of my friends and neighbours, at work inside and out of doors.

My camera was a large Graflex in which one loaded metal sheaths with cut film, four by five inches. I would have liked to develop the film myself, but the water was from a stream that was filled with peat particles, and I had no way to filter. The camera weighed ten pounds, heavy to lug, especially when I added a seventeen-inch lens. I had no light meter, and for taking my friends by their fireside, I had a problem of making them stay immobile while I guessed that a count of six would be sufficient. The results were usually good, which delighted us both. Since they had never had their photographs taken, they thought it was a miracle.

I was able to increase my small substance with selling photographs to various newspapers. I was pleased when paid ten shillings, and when one was used by the *Observer*, I was overjoyed to receive two guineas. I became ambitious: one was on the cover of the BBC magazine, *The Listener*, and several appeared elsewhere as illustrations for an article. The greatest achievement was my article on South Uist, with photographs, in the *National Geographic Magazine*. And that event prompted one unusual response. The postman arrived at Mairi MacRae's shouting, 'We have a new stamp!' A crackpot in Oregon had cut out Mairi's head from a photograph in the article and pasted it onto an envelope directed to South Uist. Enclosed was a religious tract to ask if she were saved! Since Mairi was known throughout the island, there was no difficulty at Lochboisdale post office knowing whom the letter was for.

When I had completed the book and it was all pasted up on very large, hard-backed, loose-leaf pages, I had put the photographs, which were enlarged, in as illustrations. Peigi and Mairi thought it was complete, that it was all ready. I then took it down to *Bean Iain Chlachair* with Mairi to show. There were other old ladies there having their cup of tea, sitting on the bench, turning the pages and then they all began to weep and to sob, and this distressed me. I was so upset to see this, but Mairi said, 'No, it's because they're so pleased, that's why they're crying.' And of course I showed them that these were their own songs, but they saw the photographs of husbands who had died and of their neighbours – all very vivid to them. What I found was that when they looked at a photograph or a picture, they saw far more than I ever did. They would look at a photo and see all kinds of little details that I'd never noticed. They had a marvellous eye because of course they weren't accustomed to seeing pictures even in newspapers so that when they looked at a photograph, they took in every bit of it.

Folksongs and Folklore of South Uist was well received, but one early response was not friendly. In his review in *Time and Tide*, a critic suggested that I'd been condescending to the people, insensitive to their poverty and insulting to their intelligence. The most annoying thing in the review had been the sarcastic comment that there were 'too many kelpies' in the book, by way of dismissing the cures and remedies and other customs as a deliberate embarrassment to the islanders. Of course, the word 'kelpie' is not to be found in my book: it's a word used in the Lowlands and has nothing to do with the Highlands and Islands. I said to Mairi Anndra that I'd be terribly upset if indeed I had hurt anybody's feelings. And she said: 'There's not a wrong word in the four corners of that book!' Her comment was that he was afraid I might find out about his father, a lazy man who worked at Boisdale House. It was also remembered that he'd borrowed a motorbike and wrecked it. I decided that if I ever met this critic, I would say to him, 'Was it a kelpie your father saw the night he fell off the motorbike?'

My good friend Mr Gillies, who had given me great encouragement in my efforts to collect the songs, was so delighted when *Folksongs and Folklore of South Uist* appeared, that he wrote a Gaelic poem in praise which I treasure: '. . . an ember was dying: she blew on it and brought it to life.'

DO'N TÉ A CHRUINNICH NA H-ÒRAIN
Le Fred T. Mac 'ill' Iosa

> Thàinig mi tarsuinn air uaimh an òir,
> Leabhar luachmhor bho'n a' bhean chòir;
> 'S mór an spéis, an tlachd, 's an ùidh
> Thug i do chainnt 's do cheòl Uibhist.
> An éibhleag anns an gann bha 'n deò
> Shéid i oirre, 's thug i beò a rithist;
> Maireadh a h-ainm air chuimhne
> 'Nar dùthaich, 's air taobh thall na doimhne:
> > Sin agaibh Maighread chòir,
> > Bean uasal Eilean Chanaidh.

In 1949, at the International Folkmusic Conference in Venice, I had proposed playing the recordings John and I had made on Barra but found that owing to Scotland's not being given national status, I could only get a few minutes taken off the Scottish Country Dance programme. They were doing dances on the stage, and I could see that Miss Milligan, who had brought her troop of Highland dancers, was very upset to think that she had to give up some of her time to me. So I said I wouldn't bother about it. However,

Professor Constantin Brailoiu, whom John and I had met at the Musée de l'homme the year before in Paris, asked me if I'd brought recordings and when he learned that there wasn't going to be time, he said, 'But we must hear them! You can have my time, because I only have a paper to read and it can easily be published instead in the journal.' So he gave me his hour.

When that became known, I was given the last hour of an extra day that they had added to the conference because they hadn't been able to fit in everything. On this Sunday afternoon, after everything else was completed, then my recordings were played; and by that time, when I looked down on the audience, I could see that all the English-speaking people had left. Those in the two front rows were Hungarians, Turks, and Greeks, people who were really interested in folk music. So I played my tapes. By that time I was so tired and nervous that my hand shook holding the paper so that I couldn't read it. However, the songs were wonderfully reproduced; they had a marvellous machine. The session was held in a most beautiful little theatre and was a great success.

I then had a note from Maud Karpeles, who was the secretary of the International Folkmusic Council (the first president was Vaughan Williams), saying that the famous Hungarian composer Zoltan Kodaly was coming to London and did I have any recordings to play or manuscripts to show him? I said I had. So I went to London, and I was told to meet Kodaly at half-past two the next afternoon at Boosey and Hawkes' music shop. It was a typical winter day in London – pouring cats and dogs, and black as ink. Not long after I reached the shop, the door opened and out of the rain came a man who looked as if he had just stepped out of the gutter where he had been fiddling for pennies! He had on grey spats and a very long fitted overcoat, gathered at the waist. A little tartan woollen muffler that had gone into a string stood above his coat collar and he wore a broad-brimmed black felt hat. He spoke a little French, but that was all.

We went to the back of the shop, where they had arranged a table for us. I had the wire recorder and the manuscript of my songs from South Uist. I laid them out on the table, and he had to read with his eye very close to the paper. He ran his finger back and forth; not a word was said. Then he would stop, and I would play the recordings. He listened very attentively and would shake his head, showing he approved. Then on again. This went on and on, until we were confronted by the man in charge of the shop who said he was sorry but it was half-past six and he would have to close the shop!

Shortly after that meeting with Kodaly, I had a letter from Lajos Vargyas in Hungary who wrote to ask me if I would like to contribute an article to a *Festschrift* for Bela Bartók, to be published in 1956. Of the many articles, there were, besides mine, only those of Laurence Picken from Cambridge on the 'Ritual Melodies of the T'ang Dynasty', and Maud Karpeles' paper on Cecil Sharp from Britain; all the others were from behind the Iron Curtain. And though I had published six songs from South Uist in 1943 and seven more in 1944 in the *Journal of the English Folk Dance and Song Society*, and although it was a great delight when the whole collection was at last in print with the 1955 publication of my South Uist book, still it was the peak of my happiness to have my friends' songs considered interesting enough for the Bela Bartok memorial volume, to know that the greatest of all folk music collectors was being honoured by the songs of my friends from South Lochboisdale.

CHAPTER FIVE

St Kilda, The Aran Islands, Mingulay

I FOUND WHEN I was over in Lochboisdale that the cargo ship, *The Hebrides*, from Glasgow took passengers and was going to St Kilda on the first journey since last summer. I was longing to go, and I was told to meet them at Lochmaddy the next day, and that it would cost me three pounds, ten shillings. So I hurried home with Angus John across the loch and when I got up to the cottage, I was met by Mairi Anndra: 'I hear you're going to St Kilda and it's going to cost you three pounds, ten shillings.' The seagulls or something had got there before me, over that long distance, because it was nine miles by road from the hotel.

I got my things together and went back with Angus John, took the *Loch Mor* in the evening up to Lochmaddy, spent the night there and in the early morning joined *The Hebrides*. I knew the officers and crew, tall Captain MacMillan and the First Officer, Mr Clelland, the jolly rotund Chief Steward Mr Blair, and the wireless operator Alastair MacRae who was a real authority on birds and who had taught me the constellations by pinholes in brown paper held up to the light. *The Hebrides* was a lovely ship with her red plush saloon, the long dining table in the centre; everything was always bright and shining.

Now you pass through the sound between North Uist and Harris, passing the lovely islands of Ensay, Berneray, and Pabbay, but once you get out into the Atlantic, there's always a huge swell, and this time it was an enormous oily swell, all the fifty miles across. I was on deck with my big Graflex camera and film and everything ready, but I began to feel worse and worse, and I thought, 'This is terrible; I just can't face it.' At last I had to go below to the red plush saloon and lie down. The steward came and he said, 'Now if you eat what I give you, I can cure you.' I said, 'I'll eat anything to get over this.' So he gave me a small slice of white bread soaked in Worcester sauce — Worcestershire, as we call it — and in no time I was completely cured and up on the deck and never turned a hair again. I've since been told that this sauce contains capsicum, an ingredient of seasickness remedies.

As we neared St Kilda, the sea-birds were absolutely extraordinary. Of course it was late May when there was always a tremendous number of them coming to nest. When the siren blew, they rose up in clouds — fulmars and puffins, guillemots and gannets. Near the entrance of the long horseshoe bay of Hirta, the main island, the cloud lifted and gave that vision of wild beauty that has so often been described. The small islands looked inaccessible, but Hirta itself was a most pleasing place with good pasture on its giant velvet green slope reaching to the summit of Conachair, the highest sea cliff in Britain. In the strange northern light every stone on the hillside appeared almost luminous. There was a row of houses with chimneys smoking and people with many dogs were hurrying to the shore. A group put out to meet us in a heavy rowing boat. We had brought them sad news, for a young woman who had been taken off the island some months before had died in a Glasgow hospital. A trawler had taken a message from the islands that she had appendicitis and needed hospital treatment, but too long a time elapsed before she was collected from St Kilda and the treatment came too late.

We were told that we mustn't touch a dog, because they were mangey. Nor were we to eat anything of their food. The St Kildans had had a severe winter and were terribly short, though fresh supplies were on the ship. A big rowing boat came out full of people who boarded the *Hebrides* to get news, supplies, and to talk, and we then went ashore.

We were met by a most courteous and friendly people. Some of the women wore dresses of dark blue serge, with a very tight bodice and full skirt, sometimes with an apron. Their skirts were trimmed at the foot with a little strip of black velvet and they wore a little tartan kerchief or a little shawl – not a big shawl over the head, as they did in the islands. They had boxes of knitted socks and gloves to sell, blown sea birds' eggs and rolls of the St Kilda murrit tweed. The women were the spinners and the men the weavers. The wool was from the brown or murrit sheep on the neighbouring island of Soay. This peculiar breed must have been there when the Norsemen came more than a thousand years ago, for Soay means 'sheep island' in Old Norse and such a name would not have been given unless there was something unusual about the sheep. They are more like goats than sheep, and Peigi MacRae taught me a Gaelic song beginning:

> The foot of the Hirta sheep,
> That was the nimble foot!
> That was the elegant sheep!
> The colour would grow on her back,
> She would need neither lichen nor soot,
> But spinning the wool to make trousers.

The wool of these sheep is of a colour called 'moorit', that is, dark brown; they would not need to be dyed with lichen or soot. Their fleeces are not long and shaggy, but close and thick; they have to be plucked, not shorn with shears.

I made my way along the flagstone known as 'The Street'. The houses were broad and wide with tarred roofs – superior to many I knew in South Uist. Between them were the older dwellings, built of rough stones and used as byres. The church, with the schoolhouse, the manse, the nurse's house and the little wooden post-office were at the east end of the village, while behind the houses, scattered over the hillside were the countless 'cleits', small oval-shaped stone huts with flourishing green grass tops. In these storehouses were kept dried birds, meat and feathers. The sheep on Hirta were not the Soay breed but blackface; some had double horns and I was given a pair of these as a souvenir.

There was little chance to talk to anyone because of the sad news that we brought, and the meeting with the factor and the official was attended by all adult members of the community. However, I was invited by a Mrs Gillies to come in and sit by her fire. She was wearing a most becoming tartan square on her head. I thought she must have woven it herself, but when I admired it she asked: 'Do you know Cowcaddens? That's where it came from and I can give you a nice new one.' Her own had faded to such soft and pretty colours that I said I much preferred it. This made her laugh and she took it off and gave it to me, reluctantly taking half a crown. The scarf is still a prized possession.

My great ambition was to get up the side of the hill to get photographs. There was a passenger on the ship who said he would help me with my camera, so we started off. We were joined by a St Kildan lad, who showed us where they'd had a wireless station in the '14–'18 war. A German submarine had come and given them warning that they were all to hide because they were going to blow it up, which they did. It had never been mended and they'd had no communication since that time. And this boy said, 'You see, after all you couldn't blame them. They did what we would do.'

We got to the top of Conachair to look down from this tremendous cliff, and I got my photographs. It is down these cliffs that the St Kildans went on horsehair rope to gather sea-birds and their eggs. The guillemots' eggs the St Kildans sold were perfectly beautiful, a pale greeny blue, and covered with what looks like Chinese characters in black or dark brown. But I found that their colours would fade, even if you kept them in a box.

I didn't see any ponies at all, although there were cattle and plenty of sheep. There was no transport of any kind. The May light in the Hebrides lasts until midnight, but there on St Kilda, the steep cliff made a shadow by late afternoon and the whole island was dark green velvet. It was most eerie, this silence, as we made our way back to the village. Yet when I met the resident missionary, Mr Munro, and told him what a beautiful place I thought St Kilda was he replied, 'Yes, but it's the noise; I can't stand the noise.' Well, I couldn't think what noise at all, but I suppose he meant in the winter time – the winds and gales; then, it's a very wild place.

It was St Kilda's Queen's Nurse, Miss Barclay, who told us that the people were close to starvation. She had been there a couple of years and she told me that five of the men there had duodenal ulcers. There was hardly one able to do hard physical work, and they had got so listless that they didn't cut down into the peat; they just burnt the turf on the top. The cattle were so badly fed that the milk wasn't enough for the calves and themselves, so they killed the calves and fed them to the dogs. It was essential that the dogs survived because they were needed to catch and hold the sheep so that the wool could be plucked by hand. The St Kilda dogs were not like the collies I had seen in the Hebrides. They were smooth-coated and looked like old-type lurchers.

They had no sugar, no soda, and no potatoes. The nurse did have some jam, and the children came every day for a spoonful to give them some energy. The islanders had become such beggars that the trawlermen wouldn't give them anything. The deep sea trawlers would go in to shelter and if the St Kildans went out in their small boats to ask for food, they turned the hoses on them. Once they had asked the nurse to go out in the boat. She was absolutely terrified of the small boat but they were in such desperation, they pleaded with her to go. So she did go and stood up in the boat and called to them: 'Please give us some potatoes, because we have hardly anything to eat.' So they gave her some sacks of potatoes.

*　　*　　*

That summer the authorities were deciding whether or not to take the people off the island, and the decision was made the day I visited. The land agent for the MacLeods of Dunvegan in Skye who owned St Kilda, and representatives of both the Scottish Office and the Department of Agriculture were on board the *Hebrides* to decide on the island's future. Only thirty-six persons were left and at their meeting the majority wanted to leave. The Great British Empire had never been able to provide a regular postal service and the wireless station had not been replaced.

This was in May; the inhabitants were taken off the island in August. Most of them wanted to go. The one who wanted to stay was Mr Ferguson, the postmaster, who also had charge of the tweed industry there; keeping that going was worth his while. But of all places, the Scottish Office decided to move them to Loch Aline, in Morvern, Argyllshire. They were settled there to work in the forestry service. There were no trees on St Kilda. In no time the boy who had helped me with my camera and his two sisters died of TB. Apparently, when you've been famished and are then well fed and nourished, TB is a killer.

I believe that some of the people went back to St Kilda the following summer to make more tweed, but after that the island was abandoned and the trawlermen went in and broke up the furniture to make fires. The island was sold by the MacLeods of Dunvegan to the young Marquis of Bute, who declared it a bird sanctuary. Then it was leased by the Army, who put men there to monitor rockets fired from the range on South Uist. The Army has restored cottages and built houses and made various installations. It has also built a hall and provided every possible comfort and convenience for the men stationed there, and also made a landing place for helicopters – very different to what any British government ever did for the islanders. Now it is owned by the National Trust for Scotland. Every island in the Hebrides is highly individualistic and St Kilda, being the most remote, had developed her own way of life through the centuries. It was said that they had been defeated by nature, but in my opinion she was not wholly to blame. It was the neglect of H.M. Governments.

THE ARAN ISLANDS

In 1930 I returned to New York for further lessons in theory to help me in notating the songs. I haunted the Irish Bookshop on Lexington Avenue where Miss Slattery and Mr Ferrand suffered my enthusiasm for Irish writers, history, stories, poetry, and songs. It was there that I discovered John Synge. His description of the Aran Islands made me long to visit them. There was an elderly German ship, the *Karlsruhe*, that sailed from New York to Galway, so that I could visit the Aran Islands and continue on, then, to South Uist.

I watched through the mist for the first sight of the islands as we entered Galway Bay. The little steamer, *Dun Aonghuis*, that plied between Galway and the Aran Islands was waiting at the pier. We had a calm day for the crossing. Huge creatures the crewmen called 'herring hogs' would leap out of the water and land with a tremendous splash. Galway hookers with four brown sails passed us carrying cargo. When we anchored off Inishmaan, which is between Inisheer and Inishmore, a curragh came alongside to take us ashore to the sandy beach. The sky was clear but grey, and above the white sand I could see a long line of women in brilliant red skirts and dark shawls sitting on the grey limestone. Men wearing French blue trousers and waistcoats were gathered about the black curraghs drawn up on the beach, waiting for the curragh race. These rich and clear colours against the grey limestone and the white sand made a scene like a painting of John Keating's.

I had been told that Inishmaan was where Synge had stayed and I had written to the priest that I would come and hoped he could find me accommodation, but I'd had no reply. On the shore was Father Philbin, a slight man whose hat sat lightly on the thickest bush of black hair. He remembered my letter but never thought I would appear. He took me among the women and found one who would take me, Maighread Flaherty. I was fortunate, for she radiated kindness and took me at once to her thatched white house, in a line of other such houses on the road. It was next door to the house where Synge had stayed. Maighread was young and had the beauty of the Aran women. Her wavy dark hair was parted and taken back to a thick curl between her shoulders, as was the custom. The kitchen had had so many coats of white that it shone like silver. There was a huge open fire and a dresser with a fine collection of lustre jugs and bowls. My room was off the kitchen and as white as snow. I opened the window at night and found the room thick with sea fog and my clothes damp. I had to put them in my suitcase when I went to bed and to keep my window shut.

Maighread's old father Patrick, her brother Bartley, and her niece lived in the house and in the evenings we all sat by the fire of turf and dried dung, the chimney so wide that I could see the stars. Maighread baked soda bread in an iron pot with a lid, placing it in amongst the hot embers. Potatoes were boiled and then scattered on a wide flat wicker basket to be enjoyed. Patrick told me that it was here that they hid John Blake Dillon, the Irish patriot, who was making his escape to America. And he told me of other happenings; I recognised one as the story *The Playboy of the Western World*: 'He didn't mean to kill his father – he only hit him with the hoe.' Synge, who claimed that he never made up anything, that he only wrote what he'd heard, listened from his loft above just such a fireplace as ours.

Inishmaan seemed composed entirely of giant slabs of limestone with brambles and little flowers growing in the cracks. There was little arable ground and what there was had been made by collecting soil from near the shore and adding sand and seaweed to fill the cracks. The island was covered with innumerable stone walls, making tiny fields of oats, barley, and potatoes. There was no turf (peat) on the island, so it had to be brought from Connemara in a Galway hooker which could be tied to the high stone jetty. Dried dung was also an excellent fuel to combine with the turf.

Climbing about the island on the knife-sharp limestone soon cut my shoes to pieces, so old Patrick made me a pair of pampooties from a cow hide that hung from the rafters. Cutting round my foot for the fitting with the fur side out, he then punctured holes which he threaded with fish line to tie them securely. They were rubbed with salt, so snug and soft – bliss to wear. At night, I would put them in a bucket of water to keep them from getting hard.

One Sunday, in a torrent of rain, I followed the congregation to Mass in a little church below the road, where the path descending to it had become a tiny burn which flowed right in the door. We knelt on the wet floor, so tightly packed that we nearly smothered, the steam rising from the shawls and heavy skirts. I realized the necessity of the little bell, which gave us a sign of what was happening at the altar, which we couldn't see.

Dun Conor was a short walk up the brae from the house; I was shown where Synge had his special place in the wall where he was sheltered from the wind, with a magnificent view of the Twelve Pins of Connemara, the black cliffs of Moher, County Clare, and below, the life of Inishmaan. The men were on the stone pier unloading turf, filling the creels to be carried either by donkeys or on their own backs. The curraghs out on the sea fishing and, on the road, the children shouting and playing, riding the donkeys. These children were never shy but full of fun, always laughing. Until they were nine or ten, the boys were dressed in the same red wool skirts as their mothers wore. They were not impeded; I once watched a small boy who sat at the very edge of a high cliff above a resounding surf as he baited a hook and ran the line between his toes down a hundred feet to wait for a bite.

Travel from one island to another was always by curraghs. They were made of tarred canvas over a skeleton frame and were rowed with long poles, each with a hole in the handle that fitted on a peg at the side. They rode like ducks skimming the waves but with such ease that one never felt the striking or shuddering but seemed part of the sea. The only danger was in hitting a rock or having a sharp heel puncture the skin. I watched a man take small pigs aboard, first wrapping their feet in his waistcoat.

I once shared a curragh with an American newspaper correspondent, a Miss Kelly, returning to Inishmore after a trip to Inishmaan for the day. When it came time to leave, Miss Kelly was not to be found. At long last, she appeared, but by then we had to be carried out to the curragh as it was too rough to bring it ashore. I was put in the prow where I braced myself against the sides with my elbows and held my heavy camera between my knees. When there is a fast-running tide against a strong wind, the sea between these islands becomes very rough. The two rowers with their long oars without blades sat on the narrow thwarts and shouted, '*Siubhal!* *Siubhal!*' in quickest time, never stopping an instant. The waves were high with white caps and we slid up them sideways like water beetles to the tops where I could see the hills of Connemara, then descending into the deep troughs where all was bottle green waves about us. I could hear Miss Kelly's prayers and I comforted myself with having once been told that a curragh never will capsize. At long last we were in the sheltered bay of Kilronan and I went ashore with a crick in my neck that lasted for days.

It was difficult to reach Inisheer since the *Dun Aonghuis* did not call, but I arranged to share a curragh with another visitor. It was a reasonable day with an oily swell and light wind, so the curragh had a mast with a small sail. A lad was at the tiller, which kept coming off the rudder peg so that he had to bang it down with a large stone that shook us all. It was a journey of more than two hours and we waited for the right wave to take us onto the sandy beach, the men jumping into the water to pull us up to land dry-shod. Their blue trousers were slit at the sides, to be rolled up when in water.

I was taken to a tall, slate-roofed house with a neat picket fence, where Miss O'Donnell was most welcoming and glad to have someone from the States, as she had been cook to the Lee family in Boston and was pleased to have one appreciate her art. Lobster, mackerel, salads – she even cut the potatoes into little balls to fry in deep fat. Lovely puddings too – and where she found all these delicious things on so remote an island was a miracle. Her nephew took his young sister and myself to fish for mackerel and to watch the men put the shallow half-moon net out and drag it ashore from both ends to make a fine haul of flounders and crabs.

The evenings I spent in the post office, a thatched house with a blazing fire and, beside it, a cradle of woven willow with a baby asleep. There was dancing to the accordion, and how beautiful was the postmistress – an elegant bearing, with her arms held close to her sides and her feet so nimble and neat. There was singing and I heard '*Una Bhan*', the loveliest of all Irish songs. In the freedom, the prolonging of the note, I heard in these songs the strong resemblance to the old Scots Gaelic songs I was hearing in Barra and South Uist, especially the waulking songs.

Inishmore, the biggest of the islands, was a contrast to the others, with a pier and the little town of Kilronan with a small hotel, many slate-roofed houses, and a shop. I stayed in the guest house where they were accustomed to visitors from many countries. Many were the students who came to study Irish and acquire the *blas*, or smooth accent.

There was a good road for nine miles through fertile fields. Everywhere there were exciting places to see, from prehistoric to Christian times. The guide I found to take me in his side-car about the island was Pat Mullen who was a friend to me for the rest of his long life. He was very proud of his lively and handsome grey horse and as we came to his field, Pat would whistle and the horse would lift his head high, arch his tail and gallop in circles. Pat knew all the famous sites. I especially wanted to see the site of St Enda's Monastery at Killeany, which was founded in the sixth century and gave the name 'Aran of the Saints' to the islands. The scholars and missionaries were trained there to Christianise Europe. And then there were the prehistoric forts at the edge of the high cliffs

– enormous, with no real evidence of their origin. They would need a big population to build them, and who would be the invaders to storm these mighty walls?

The privilege I had from Pat Mullen was in listening to his folktales. He was well over six feet, powerful and agile. He could have lived with joy in the Fingalian world. I quote from a letter written to me in 1967, not long before he died.

> *The feeling comes to me that I must go back to the time of long ago when, one might say, the world was young and great deeds were done by the many great heroes of our race. I cannot explain to you, dear friend of mine, how passionately I revel in retelling those tales and thinking of them with emotion. You see (whether it is a fault or not) all the scenes and actions depicted in any or all the tales come in plain pictures for my mind to see and I have lived through them all like as if I was there myself and had seen an actual happening. I suppose one can find but few story tellers today whose minds can jump back to the old Folk Days and live himself in the story while telling it.*
>
> *Yes – even now I can see the Dolav Dhura, Monarch-of-the-World's Son, who while fighting bravely and killing many champions on the Ventry Harbour Strand, heard a wild cry and looked to see Morneal's son Gual hurrying to the fray. One look he, Dolav Dhura, took then he said, 'Ah, he has come! And now when all shall soon be over what Bard shall ever put me in his Book of Fame?'*

MINGULAY

In the Lochboisdale Hotel I met a Mr Russell, an Englishman who had been sheep farming in Montana for many years and had returned to buy the three southernmost islands of the Long Island to continue his sheep farming. All three – Pabbay, Mingulay, and Bernera, known as Barra Head – were uninhabited, except for the lighthouse keepers on Barra Head. Mingulay had been evacuated twenty years before, the people having resettled on the island of Vatersay which was not so remote. There was a fine stone church, which included the priest's house, and a small schoolhouse. The other houses had lost their thatched roofs and all that was left were the stone walls and the stone querns in which the islanders had ground their oats. Mr Russell asked me to come to Mingulay where I could photograph the splendid cliffs with the many varieties of sea-birds and assist with the cooking for his two shepherds and himself who lived in the schoolhouse.

To reach this island I had to go to Barra's port, Castlebay, and then take the lighthouse boat which sailed once a fortnight with supplies, calling at Mingulay. Going ashore was difficult – getting into the small dinghy to reach the landing place of perpendicular rocks. There was usually a swell and one had to jump at the precise moment to land on the flat rock, to be seized by the shepherd, and scramble up the path. The boatman who rowed the dinghy had a stutter which was increased under tension; by the time he said 'jump!' it was past the rise of the swelling wave and so it meant waiting while we pushed away from the rocks and rode in again on the crest. There was not only myself to go ashore but my camera and boxes of food, mail, and a cat in a basket. These all had to be grabbed by the man on the rocks the instant the dinghy rose.

The cooking was no problem. The coal stove had an oven, which was sometimes hot enough for baking. A whisky bottle was the rolling pin for my oatcakes and there was plenty of milk from the two nanny goats. The eggs were from the cliffs – from gulls, guillemots and razor-bills – good for custards and omelettes but never to be boiled, when the taste would be of foul fish. Spam was made interesting in many ways and then we had rabbits which were caught by a pair of ferrets, the treasured friends of Mr Russell who could pet and handle their wild jumping play as though they were harmless pussies. I was with the shepherds in not daring to touch them.

The men would take me with my heavy Graflex and a movie camera to the top of the high cliffs where the thousands of sea-birds were nesting and flying below us. They sounded exactly like the children on the East Side of New York, playing in the streets, murmuring, shouting, squealing – a terrific noise. I got my movie camera set up in a very perilous position to take guillemots which were across a deep divide in the cliff opposite. Just as I got the camera focused, a stone fell and killed a guillemot right on its ledge. It never even fell off, a reminder of God and the sparrow.

Mr Russell, the shepherds, and I were all to go to Barra Head, the next island south where the lighthouse is, to count the sheep. Since we were to be away for three days, it was necessary to take the two nanny goats which would need to be milked. When the fishing boat arrived for us, the goats bolted and would not be caught. The *Little Flower* wouldn't wait, so I volunteered to stay on Mingulay, as I could milk the goats when they returned in the evening. 'I don't mind staying alone and I can look after myself.' So they reluctantly went off.

Now it was midsummer, so it was light all night and beautiful weather. That evening I went out to get the goats. Mr Russell had said that if you took a pan of their food (he had very special food for them) and rattled it, these two wretched goats would come. Well I rattled the pan and called. I opened the gate which led into a kind of compound, but nothing would bring them. I then got a stick and called and tried to round them up. Not a bit of it. They just flew off. Then I took the stick and began to damn and employ a vocabulary that I never use and with that, the goats came. Obviously, that was the command they'd been used to. They ran in the barn and got up on their little benches so it was very easy for me to milk them.

Mr Russell had five big cats and when I went into the house to make my supper of scrambled birds' eggs and goat's milk, the cats came in, one by one, and sat on the bench in silence. It made me think of the story of the man who enters a lonely cottage, and a big cat comes in and looks at him and says, 'Has Martin came yet?'

The man doesn't know what to reply, but pretty soon another big cat comes in and says to him, 'Has Martin came yet?' 'No!' And then another big cat comes in and sits down and says, 'Has Martin came yet?' 'NO!' 'Well then,' screamed the first one, 'I'm King of the Cats.' They sat there and stared at me, so serious and important that I felt small among them. However, I gave them their supper, and they settled down. I had my three days, and I think I'm the only woman who ever stayed alone on Mingulay.

CHAPTER SIX

Barra, Nova Scotia

SOUTH UIST IN those days was famous for pipers. They played so well that no matter where you heard piping at games and competitions, it never compared with South Uist. This was because the Uist men had had Pipe Major John MacDonald of Inverness as their teacher; he was the greatest authority on pibroch, the classical music of the Highland bagpipe. Pibroch is very involved and difficult, a matter of theme and variations, ornamented by complicated grace notes, all of which have to be played absolutely correctly.

Pipe Major MacDonald was in business as a traveller for Younger's, the brewery, and he travelled all over Scotland, but his firm let him off for two or three months in the winter time. Finlay Mackenzie at the Lochboisdale Hotel put him up and arranged that he should carry on his teaching. Everybody delighted in having him.

Pipe Major MacDonald was very kind to me. I was thrilled by pipe music, and he let me sometimes sit in at a lesson he was giving. I would go over from Glendale to the Lochboisdale Hotel, where he used to give lessons in a little back smoking-room. You know how people say, 'I cannot stand a piper playing in a room; I can't bear it.' But these young men, his pupils, played so beautifully that you could be in a room with them and enjoy it. And of course they had an enormous repertoire of reels, strathspeys, marches and pibrochs. He played the violin, and I used to accompany him at the Broadwood piano that had been given to Finlay Mackenzie when he was married and which was kept in good tune.

One rainy night when the *Lochearn* had come in from Barra, a young man came into the room where we were playing, and Finlay Mackenzie introduced him as young Campbell of Inverneill. Now we stopped playing and asked him if he played the piano, and he said, 'No, but I can play any wind instrument,' and I thought, 'What conceit!' But I found in later years that he *could* play any wind instrument. He said to me, 'I hear you take photographs, and I would like some for a book that Compton Mackenzie and I are writing. The proceeds are to go to the fishermen, to the Sea League.' So I said yes, I would send him some, and that was the end. I was meant to leave that night and I would have missed him, but I had a very, very bad cold and had been told to stay and wait till the next night. And he had been held up, so that he had to come to South Uist unexpectedly. So it was strange that we just happened to meet that time.

Now when I went down to Oxford, I told my good friends the MacGregors that I'd met this young man who wanted photographs for a book, and I would have to decide what to send him. Duncan said, 'No, no, don't send him anything! I know the kind; he'll never pay you anything.' And he never did!

John Campbell then phoned in the spring and asked me to come over to Barra to Northbay, where he had a house, and he was going to have other friends, Gaelic speakers, to stay for the week, and I said to Mairi Anndra, 'I think I'd like to go.' And she said very truly, 'Your Gaelic isn't good enough.' However, I went and it was all very interesting. I didn't have to speak at all. He would say, 'We'll take our lunch and the rest of them can work, and we'll go for a walk.' The lunch was always wholemeal bread which was very hard to chew, and there was a mixture of whisky with Crabbie's ginger wine and water in a flask for our dram. The bread was buttered, but that was about all. He had a little car and we would drive to a very beautiful place, and we'd start off to go along the beach. He had a butterfly net and would soon disappear, and I wouldn't see him again until he'd reappear for lunch. We would eat our pieces of bread with our dram, and then he'd disappear again. But I found out in time that this is how he lives and enjoys, and he expects you to do the same thing. Why walk along yacketing when there's really nothing much to say, except to admire the view? Each to his own.

In 1935, John came to America and was with me at Glenshaw for a month or more, working on what was to be *The Book of Barra*, written with Compton Mackenzie. He never once, to me or to anyone else, showed the slightest interest in my own self. Either he was completely engrossed in his book or he was collecting moth cocoons in the woods. My aunt and uncle and everybody else were puzzled why in the dead of winter he had nothing better to do than to come to Glenshaw from Scotland to work at his typewriter from dawn to dark. And it wasn't until the day before he left, in the evening when we went for a walk – it was March by then and the road was slush – down towards the bridge and back that he asked me to marry him. 'Well,' I said, 'I think you'd better go back to Barra and think this over seriously, to be sure.' And he said, 'Oh, I think I'm sure.' We didn't say anything coming back.

The next day we went in to see my Uncle George, who was a very important attorney, and told him. And he said, 'Very nice. My motto for a happy marriage is "Bear and Forbear".' He was never enthusiastic about anything, but he was pleased, and he had recognised in John a scholar and an unusual young man.

We then went down to Aunt Elsie's where we had dinner, and afterwards John was put on the night train to New York. I waited until the next day and then went back to Glenshaw in the evening and walked into the kitchen where my sisters were all standing with their husbands, and announced, 'I'm going to marry John Campbell.' They were absolutely amazed; they had no conception that anything like this was in mind. It gave me a private satisfaction.

We were married in Glasgow in the manse of John's great friend, Revd Calum MacLeod. It was from 'Uncle Fred' Moir's house, 16 Kensington Gate, and he was my sponsor – a noble patriarch in his eighties with his soft white beard. I could not have had a more distinguished companion, nor one I would more willingly have had with me on this anxious journey. On hearing that it was to be in Gaelic, he asked for a translation so as to be sure I was properly wed. He hired a limousine and pinned two lovely white orchids to my jacket. The minister's wife was the only other witness, and all that was required of me was to say *Tha*, meaning *yes*. It was very serious, just the kind of wedding everyone ought to have.

We spent our honeymoon in the Lofoten and Vesteraalen Islands, situated off the coast of Norway and, like the Hebrides, much dependent on sea fishing. John was very interested in the fishermen's troubles which arose from the fact that the Minch, the inland sea between the Inner and Outer Hebrides, was open to English trawlers. On their return from the Northern Icelandic fishing grounds, they would trawl for their last catch before reaching their ports, with the result that they took fish which the crofter fishermen depended on for their living and for their food.

Compton Mackenzie, then living on Barra, had founded the Sea League which John had joined as an enthusiastic supporter, later becoming its secretary and the editor of its journal. The League, made up of fishermen from all over the Hebrides, wanted to persuade Parliament to close the Minch to trawlers. They got nowhere, since there was no interest in the worries of the Hebrideans – and besides, there were MPs whose constituencies were the English fishing ports. We wanted to see how things were handled in Norway where a wise and generous government had treated the Lofoten Islanders very well.

After leaving the Lofotens and the Vesteraalens, we returned to Bergen on the *Princesse Rognvald*, one of the large comfortable ships on coastal service. From there to Oslo by train to meet John's friends, Professors Marstrander, Sommerfelt and Borgstrøm, well known for their interest in Hebridean Gaelic studies; then on to Copenhagen for two days; then by sea to Stettin in Germany, to travel by Berlin to see John's mother at Marienbad in Czechoslovakia, a famous spa for restoring strength and reducing weight after high living, to be ready for the next 'season'. It was in 1935 at the time Hitler was making much of the 'Sudeten problem'; sympathy was expressed for the Sudeten Germans. I was told that the Czechs had no aristocracy!

I had long wanted to see Germany, Bonn especially, for Beethoven. We changed trains in Berlin on our way to Marienbad, and that hot day removed all my desire. The station was crowded, and all were greeting each other with right arm upraised, shouting 'Heil Hitler!' There was a stench of evil that put fear in me. I was glad to return to Scotland, which we did travelling through Holland.

John had bought a 38-foot motor yacht with a lugsail called the *Assynt*, which was lying at Dundee on the east coast of Scotland. He had two fishermen bring her to St Andrews, where she was repainted black, red and white, and renamed the *Gille Brighde*, the Gaelic name of a shore bird which has these colours and which is called the oyster-catcher in English. It was then brought through the mid-Scotland canal to a yard in Glasgow near the Buchanan Street railroad station, where its engine was overhauled.

Most of the money from our wedding presents was spent on making it comfortable and, after our honeymoon, we came back to Glasgow and boarded the yacht. With the help of one hand, John MacNeil, we sailed from there down a filthy canal, through the slums of Glasgow, and eventually emerged out into the Clyde. We went across and spent the first night at Port Glasgow, where we could have safe anchorage. Now big ships came up the Clyde, and they made us roll, so that I actually fell out of my bunk. It was all very smelly and not very attractive. However, it was going to be down the Clyde and out into the beauties of the Highlands and Islands the next day. And so we started.

We'd bought a new water tank at large expense which was fastened on the deck in a safe place. We saw a great black cloud coming up the Clyde, and this proved to be a very smart and swift storm, so we bucketed and ploughed and pitched, and I saw the water tank go overboard. I didn't dare say anything in case they tried to turn to get it, which would have been a disaster. We had a fearful sail; it was so bad that I couldn't go below. I just had to sit tight and hold on, and eventually we got to Rothesay, on the Isle of Bute, and tied up at the mooring. John, and John MacNeil then went ashore to buy a dinghy, and I went below to find that everything we possessed was on the floor. There was a great mixture of tea and condensed milk, and my beautiful box of Elizabeth Arden lotions and whatnot were all mixed together on top of the bedding. I had to stay to clean this up because they said they couldn't stop; it was very important for them to get the dinghy. I got the cabin reasonably clean and when they returned with the dinghy, we set off for the Crinan Canal.

John's aunts, whom I'd never met, lived at Inverneill on Loch Fyne, and when we'd got through the Crinan, he phoned them. They were simply delighted that they were going to meet me, and it was arranged that they would come the next morning. And so the next day we rose early. I was standing in my panties and bra, combing my hair, when I looked up through the skylight to see the faces of two elderly ladies looking down on me; whereupon I dived into the little galley, where you had to bend double to get in, and pulled on the rest of my clothes to emerge out on deck. They were very gracious and very pleasant. They had a car, so we drove to see Iverneill and Taynish where John had lived as a boy.

We sailed on from there in the most beautiful weather. The sun was setting, and all the sea was gold as we came to Oban where we anchored – but no, we mustn't go ashore at Oban; we must hurry on because we had the whole of the Minch to cross. So we left very early in the morning, about five o'clock, and going through the Sound of Mull reached Tobermory where they had to get oil for the engine and other supplies. So we tied up at the big pier and the two Johns disappeared.

Now a cruise ship called the *King George V*, taking people to Iona, used to come by Tobermory and then on around the north of Mull, stopping at Staffa and Iona; or else they would do the reverse route. This morning they were coming up and Tobermory was the first stop. There was a crowd of people standing on the pier looking down on me and a great number of beautiful white yachts all around me because it was a regatta day. The pier-master with a big brown spade beard leaned over and said to me, 'You must move along because the "George" is coming'. And with that, I heard a whistle, and a thing that looked as big as the *Queen Mary* was rapidly approaching. 'Well,' I said, 'I *can't* start the engine!' (It was a big Kelvin engine, and you had to swing a handle, which is very hard to do.) And the pier-master with his beard said, 'Don't worry, don't worry. I'll untie you and you'll just shift along, and you'll be all right.' So he untied the ropes, and I was trying to push off and doing this I caught two fingers of my right hand in the rope. I never even felt it at the time, and I just moved out from underneath the prow of this enormous monster.

In the meantime, the yachts – all painted with flags up and so on – were terrified that I was going to bump them, so they were all shouting, and I looked up at this mob of men and said, 'Will one of you give me a hand?' Not one moved. But an Englishman in a Panama hat, well at the back of the crowd, cried, 'I'll help you!' And he rushed down and got in his dinghy at the little jetty beside the pier to come out to me. Whereupon John, and John MacNeil, hearing the *George* blowing and blowing for me to move away, came rushing down and said to the man, 'No, it's all right, we'll go.' And so they rowed out and shouted to me, 'Drop the anchor, drop the anchor!' Now the anchor was brand-new and the chain was nicely coiled round and round, and the anchor was on the top. So I pushed over the anchor, and then I realised something very important: it wasn't fastened, and my fingers were absolutely numb. They were useless. I couldn't hold the anchor, and I couldn't do anything, so it just was flop down, bang and rattle, rattle rattle, rattle, plop! I went below and stretched out on a bunk and opened a book. I soon heard voices and the hatch opened and the two of them looked down. They saw my face and the book, and they never said one word; they just shut the hatch. They moved the yacht over to another pier on the far side of the bay and tied alongside.

I, in my silent fury, was trying to make lunch in the little galley where I couldn't stand upright: I had to open the hatch and put my head out before I could stand up straight. I had a little Tilley stove to cook on. Now through this hole came little bits of coal – a little bit of coal, and pretty soon another little bit of coal. I had seen among all that mob of men on the pier Mr MacCall, the Exciseman from South Uist and Lochboisdale, whom I knew pretty well. So I put my angry head out of the hatch and there was Mr MacCall.

'Hello, there! You don't know your old friends!'

'You didn't know yours when I was calling for help!'

'Oh well, I could see you'd be all right!'

Mr MacCall was at home, being a *Muileach*, since they are Macleans and Mull is the country of the Macleans. I could understand the feuds of the old days when an affront would bring their enemies to burn the town. If this had happened at Lochboisdale, any man would have helped. They would never see a woman stuck in such a situation, no matter who she was, without helping her at once.

Early the next morning at low tide they retrieved the anchor with a boat hook and we started off across the Minch to Barra.

John thought we could just live on this yacht. There was this great thing in its favour: it had a WC. Also we had very good lamps and very good bunks, and except for the four-foot high galley, the yacht was very comfortable. John was finishing *The Book of Barra*, and this was very important to him, so I read and amused myself while he typed away, littering the floor with pages torn out of the typewriter. We were anchored in Northbay, Barra. It was late in the season and the equinoctial gales were coming, and I realised that there was a good wind blowing and a storm coming up. What I noticed was that the Catholic church would go whizz past the porthole, and then again I would see it go whizz past the porthole, and then again I would see it go whizz past the porthole, nearer and nearer. And I said, 'this isn't good; I think we're dragging the anchor.'

'Oh, you always think we're dragging the anchor. No, no, we're perfectly safe. Now I must get on with this.'

Whizz again. 'I don't like it; the Church looks too near.'

'There's nothing the matter; you're always worried about something.'

However, I went up on deck and just in time to grab a boat-hook and keep us from ramming the *Star of the Sea*, a huge fishing boat which was lying in the bay. Then I saw on the shore three men. I couldn't hear because of the wind, but I could see their mouths opening wide as they threw their arms in the air, jumping and dancing to warn us. With that, John did come up, and we had to get the typewriter and all his manuscript and a few things into the dinghy at great peril, because the sea was extremely rough, and row to the shore.

I was never so happy in my life to put my feet on land, and we didn't go back. We'd had six weeks, at least, of life on a yacht, which is all very well in lovely weather, but in storms when you're continually having to watch to see if you're dragging the anchor or what's happening, it's a miserable life.

So we moved into a corrugated iron house where Compton Mackenzie had been living while his own was being built further up the road.

This little house had been a shop. It had two rooms in the front and two little ones at the back, and upstairs two more rooms –

all very primitive. There were oil lights and candles. There was no water. The spring was some way down the road, but we had the pleasure of a chemical W.C. We painted the walls and made bookshelves.

I had been given five hundred dollars by my Uncle George Shaw, and I was determined that I was going to have a Steinway grand piano. I went with John to Glasgow to buy it at Patersons, where we met his aunt, Mrs Stewart of Fasnacloich. As we looked at these wonderful pianos, she said, 'But my dear, you can buy a perfectly good piano for six pounds, an upright, and surely this isn't necessary.' And I said yes, it was very necessary to me. It was the desire of my life. So the grand piano was sent out by steamer to Castlebay and then brought by lorry around to our little tin house. The room was quite big enough for it. We had an open fire and lovely rugs on the floor, and it became a drawing-room of which we were very proud. It always amused me to see my American relations and other newly-arrived friends looking with horror at the kind of shack we were living in, and then walking in and seeing this lovely room.

Our landlord was John MacPherson, known as 'The Coddy', whom I had met when I came to Barra on my travel by bicycle through the Long Island. He welcomed me as a friend and told me that he had doubted if he would ever see his map again, but to his surprise it had been returned from Paris. The Coddy was postmaster and his office also had the shop. His wife was an angel of kindness and help while he was the best of landlords. Our little coal stove in the livingroom was taken away and a fine stone fireplace built. His Christmas present was a wild goose. For John, he was the teller of the folk tales which became the classic *Tales Told by The Coddy*.

Among the Barra friends who were telling John Gaelic stories was Miss Annie Johnston, a native of Barra whose knowledge of songs and stories was fathomless. I had known her from my days in South Uist when she came to judge the *Mod* in Daliburgh. I had visited her house in Castlebay where she was schoolteacher, and she had taken me to hear singers, especially the old women famous for their *luadhadh* or waulking songs which were sung when the blankets or tweed were taken from the loom to be shrunk, with many hands handing the length of cloth around a long table, pounding it at each point. There was one ancient song about the rivalry of a Barra woman and a Uist woman, and I could even sense that rivalry, for Barra was a prosperous island compared to Uist which was poor, and the Uist folk were called the *rogallaich*, meaning 'the shaggy or hairy ones'.

Annie Johnston was the most fascinating teller of ghost stories and fairy tales, and one evening she told me of the Vatersay light. And then, one black night, when we were walking down the road, suddenly she said, 'There's the Vatersay light!' It was like the light of an electric torch, a round light which ran along the shore of Vatersay. It stopped for a second and then ran again, then went out, then came on again and came back. We stood and watched it. It could easily have been a single car lamp which went along, but where this light ran along the shore there was no road, no track, no house, nothing. The Vatersay light was seen every now and then, but there was no explanation. Just a round ball of light; it ran along in the dark on the edge of the shore and could never be explained. The saying is in Barra today that ever since a military plane crashed on the hill of Vatersay and all the four men were killed, the Vatersay light has never been seen. Well, whatever it is, I did see this extraordinary thing, for which there is absolutely no explanation. It was too big to be St Elmo's Fire.

John's reason for living on Barra was to improve his colloquial Gaelic, to achieve the *blas*. And he also wanted to be near his friend, Compton Mackenzie, whom he'd known since 1933, first through correspondence about John's book, *Highland Songs of the Forty-five*, poems and translations of the famous Gaelic poets of that period. They were writing *The Book of Barra* together, had founded the Sea League, and were publishing a newspaper with that name.

I didn't know Compton Mackenzie at that time at all. John had never said that he was going to marry anybody, and so when he sent word that he'd returned, I felt very much out of it. I felt I wasn't welcomed; in fact, I knew I wasn't, and so it was uncomfortable. At the same time, I realised that Compton was very necessary to John.

Compton was a born actor; his family on both sides had been actors for generations, the Batemans in America and the Comptons in Britain. His grandfather, going on stage, had changed his name from Mackenzie to Compton; Compton had brought back the 'Mackenzie'. Compton had great charm; he was very handsome, amusing and erudite. But he was an actor, and everywhere he stood was a stage. He had loads of friends, and he held open house. The people on Barra adored him. He didn't own Barra, as is often said, but he did buy a small piece of property, *Suidheachan*, which means 'the sitting down place', and it was very well-named, because everyone stopped there to sit. When his wife came to stay, Faith Compton Mackenzie, I asked her to come to tea. When she arrived, she saw my grand piano and at once we began to play for each other. She was tall, elegant, Italian-looking, beautiful – and as soon as she sat down at the piano, you knew that she was a born pianist. We played duets; our best efforts were the overtures of Beethoven, Rossini and Mozart. I heard that when she went back to *Suidheachan*, she told them that I wasn't quite the odd creature they'd thought and that I did have some respectable attributes. Faith became a great friend and was so until she died. In later years she came to Canna several times, and she wrote her novel, *The Crooked Wall*, in our house.

Years after, Compton moved to Edinburgh – 31 Drummond Place – a lovely Georgian house. Once when I was down for the Festival and had been staying with Faith and Compton, I had to catch an early morning train (4.35) to get back to Canna. I was planning to go to a hotel or even to wait in the station, but Compton said, 'No, you come and sit by the fire in the study with me, because

I'm working. (He was a great night owl.) 'You wait there, and we'll call a taxi.' So I went in and sat by the fire, and he said, 'You know, Margaret, when we lived in Barra, you didn't like me.' And I said, 'You didn't like me either.' And we both laughed, and I said, 'There's one thing I said from the beginning, and that was that you were the greatest influence for good with John, and I've always been grateful because you gave him confidence and you made him work. For that I have always been grateful.' And from that time on, after that conversation in his Edinburgh study, we were great friends.

NOVA SCOTIA

John decided that we should visit Nova Scotia and Cape Breton Island. He had spent a short time there in 1932 at the St Francis Xavier University in Antigonish. The President, Dr P.J. Nicholson, Professor of Physics and a noted Gaelic scholar, had encouraged him to return, for the descendants of the Barra people had a great store of Gaelic songs and stories waiting to be collected. So in 1937, we sailed on the *Duchess of Montrose* for Quebec, taking our little Vauxhall car and a primitive recording machine that used wax cylinders.

We crossed the St Lawrence river by ferry for the long drive south through Nova Scotia. It was extremely hot, a contrast to the cool of the Hebrides; we kept from melting with a giant thermos flask of iced Coca Cola. Our route followed a wide river where men were guiding huge rafts of logs to a pulp mill. When we stopped at a lonely petrol station, I was horrified to see a grinning young man hold up by its stub tail a beautiful bob-cat for me to admire. A big mistake! What fascinated our onlookers were the yellow 'flippers' on our English car that would suddenly appear to signal our turns.

A ferry took us across the Gut of Canso to Cape Breton, another country. We first called on a friend of John's, Jonathan G.

MacKinnon at Whycocamagh, once editor of a Gaelic newspaper, *MacTalla* (*Echo*). He advised us to make our headquarters at Baddeck, a little town on the Bras d'Or lake. There we found the perfect little private hotel owned by a Mr Fraser who was pleased to have us.

Dr Nicholson had given us the name of a Mrs Catherine Patterson whose mother's people had come from Barra. She was the greatest find, a friend at once, and she had many songs which she sang in a clear, true voice. She led us to many singers, and so we travelled from Christmas Island to Glace Bay, filling our cylinders with rare songs and stories. They were so like our friends in Barra that we felt we had never left home. Their Gaelic and knowledge of that island after three generations was such that you would have thought they had recently arrived.

So many pretty towns and villages with names such as Boisdale, Castlebay, Barra Head, Iona, and fine farms with neat white houses, but the dense stretches of forest showed what the early settlers had confronted. I saw one abandoned farm where a fir tree was springing through the porch. I felt that scene sinister, as though the forest was determined to take back its lost land.

We were sorry to leave these new friends, so kind and generous in giving us the happiest hospitality, and filling our cylinders with valuable songs and stories. When we arrived back in Barra, our friends there were as excited as ourselves when listening to the songs. Many were familiar, though perhaps with new verses or a change in the tune. They were eventually transcribed to appear in John's book, *Songs Remembered in Exile*, which gives an account of why the Barra people had to leave their island and describes their life on Cape Breton.

CANNA'S BASALT CRAGS

To their grey heights they rise,
The basalt crags thus far into blue air
Stayed where force into form no farther lifted
Archaic columns of fire frozen to stone
Temple where winds will sing, clouds gather
Till sun and ice of summers and winters totter
Their rocky hexagons. In vein and crevice
Wild bees find sweetness of wild thyme
Whose fine roots infasten crystal by crystal, grain by grain
Boulders that tumble
Down slope whose stunted hazel leans to the prevailing weather.
Geometric unseen shapers limn
Wind-rounded waterworn contours of the isles
To the least lens winter-green moss turns to the sun
And bend of sedge a-quiver in current of air that lifts
Seabirds as rock-face turns gale from its course.
What part in this Concord of wisdom's unerring agents by whose
    design
Fall of fartherest star by ever so little mountain and grass-blade
    stirs,
Sand-grain and rain-drop poised to fall
To the wet hill's trickling water-track, has a thought
That stays no tempest, leaves no trace
Of seer on seen, and yet knows all?

                                        Kathleen Raine

CHAPTER SEVEN

Canna

JOHN'S DEGREE AT Oxford was in Rural Economy and his ambition was to find a farm he could bring back; he wanted most of all to own an island – to make it bloom, so to speak. When Canna came on the market – it was The Coddy who told him about it – he saw his chance. He went at once to Canna with his lawyer and cattle-valuator, and clinched the deal then and there. This was in April 1938, while I was away in hospital in Edinburgh. He came and stood in the door looking very serious: 'I've bought the Island of Canna.'

I had to remain in hospital and then a long convalescence, so that I could not be there to help with the packing of china, pictures, innumerable books, as well as the furniture, including the grand piano. All was transported by our large fishing boat with the help of our sailor friend, John MacNeil, from Barra to Canna, some fifty miles across the Minch.

I arrived at the end of August on a lovely day, delighted to find that Canna had a proper pier, then up the road to the gate to see huge trees, flower beds, and the big stone house coated in thick ivy. It had a melancholy air, as though the home of sick Brontës. The views from the windows and the garden were lovely, but inside was another story. I wasn't in the parlour for ten minutes before I'd taken the coal scuttle outside on the lawn. It was all rusted, a cast iron affair, with an octagonal lid, in the middle of which was a Greek goddess painted on glass that was all cracked. I took that right out the door, and then I began to explore the house.

There were piles of mattresses by the half-opened windows, and the cats had come in. We had to burn things and scour and clean. They had used our lovely antique mahogany table to stand on in their tackety boots while unloading the boat. There were marks that couldn't be cleaned, but when I said, 'Look at those marks all over where you've been standing and the drop-leaf is broken,' John MacNeil said, 'Oh, we can put that right at once.' So they turned the table over and put the wing down and screwed it in so that the screws went right out the other side. That made me roar with laughter, and I took all following calamities with ease.

We had to buy the Thoms' furniture with the house, but it was so worm-eaten that we hardly could keep a piece of it, except one cabinet. There were very few books in it, but there were colour photographs of the Royal Family, including Queen Elizabeth as a baby, all thumbtacked in the back of it. Ebony whatnots were screwed to the wall with dreadful little statues and seaside mementoes. The parlour was festooned with long lace curtains and little baubles on the mantelpiece. There were tables covered with red plush glued on and then handmade lace tacked all around it – and underneath *piles* of sawdust from the woodworms. The greatest find was in the attic, a John Broadwood square piano of 1835 and now in perfect condition.

There were only candles and lamps. The bench in the kitchen hall, where the boots are now, held all the lamps, and you had to trim the wicks and clean the shades and watch that you didn't turn them up too high. The Thoms had had maids for this chore, but I was well-accustomed from Barra. First we had gas light, at the start of the war, and then in 1950–51, we got our first electricity and that ran with petrol. Early on John said, 'Do you realise this light costs us half a crown an hour?' We didn't dare turn it on half the time. At long last we had a generator that used diesel oil so we could now have a refrigerator, and central heating for some of the rooms.

There was an old-fashioned range which had been put in the year before. It was terrible for the cooks, but the Thoms wanted the same kind as they'd always had. It took so long, and it didn't heat the ovens properly. Their cook, Kate MacLeod, had had to start the fire at 3 a.m. in the morning in order for Mr Thom to have his bath. We removed this museum piece and replaced it with an Esse Premier. It had three ovens, always at the desired heat. The Esse had a long life, and we've had nothing like it since.

There was the great luxury of two bathrooms and the wonder to me were the bath tubs, made of wood, long and deep. They were painted white and the water stayed hot, not like the enamel metal tubs. Unfortunately, it was found that the wood had started to deteriorate, and, though I begged to have it restored, I was told that before long it might give way and one would land in the dining room. So modern tubs were installed. There was also a Sitz-bath, a museum piece which has remained in the bathroom, a relic of the first Mr Thom.

The Thoms were interested in birds and kept careful records of sightings. If they didn't recognise a bird, they shot it to identify it later. Annie MacLeod, the dairy maid, told about a bird flying in the window at the Square, and they didn't know what it was. 'Didn't you ask the Thoms?' I asked, knowing they kept a list of birds. 'Oh, no. They'd have killed it.'

There were cases of stuffed birds lining the walls of the billiard room and running along the walls of both the downstairs and upstairs halls. We still have a few of them. The spoonbill on the desk in the front hall is one. But we burned thirty-two of them on the shore. They had to be carted out in a barrow. There was a raven, pale blue with mould; an albatross whose feathers were falling out, with one glass eye. A seal in a case in the front hall presented a study of the moth, from the larvae to the little moths themselves.

We made a greenhouse with glass from the bird cases, against the back wall of the garden. The mistake in building it there was that the wall was filled with slaters – woodlice, which have hard little shells – impossible to get rid of. I had to stand all my seed trays in water to keep the slaters from eating the plants. Otherwise, in one night, all the little seedlings would be gone. I had tomato plants, but the rats came and ate them, so I gave up. However, I grew all the vegetables in the garden. And the Thoms had planted apple and plum trees, and five varieties of gooseberries.

We had the ivy taken off the walls, the dwelling place of millions of blue-bottles and the access to the windows for the rats. This was a great improvement to the appearance of the house, and it lost its gloom. The escalonia had been planted as a hedge on either side of the path up to the house. Eventually we just let it grow until it formed a tunnel which of course is a refuge when you come in from the road in a fierce gale.

My mother-in-law came to see the house soon after we arrived and announced that she would provide curtains. A huge album of patterns arrived from famous decorators in London, with magnificent materials of damask and velvet, and heavy brocades, to choose the curtains for the drawing-room. It happened that at this time I had found on the road a very large green caterpillar with red trimmings. I deposited it carefully under a candy box lid on the hall table to wait for John to identify, but when I lifted the lid that evening it had gone. We searched high and low, but it had disappeared.

A few days later I received a letter from the decorators asking for the return of their pattern book. When I lifted it from the table in the drawing-room, I found attached to the little fringes of the material a splendid cocoon of many colours, still soft. I wrote to say what had happened, and that when the cocoon was firm, I could detach it with no harm to the materials. They sent an understanding letter, and when the cocoon was ready, I removed it with ease and sent off their album. A beautiful Puss Moth (*D. vinula*) emerged eventually. The marvel was the strength of the caterpillar, to lift the lid and travel the long distance, down from the table, crossing carpets and floor, mounting the other table to find the most exquisite material to make his bed.

By degrees, we settled in at Canna House. John's family and mine come together in the dining room in an interesting way. I was named for a Margaret Fay who was Mrs Samuel Brown of Vermont. She was a direct descendent of Stephen Fay – his great-granddaughter, I believe – who had the Catamount Tavern in Old Bennington on the Hill where Ethan Allen and The Green Mountain Boys gathered. Stephen Fay's son was the surgeon. The battle of Bennington was very vivid to her, the whole story. When she died, Grandma Brown, as we called her, left me the tea set that had been in Catamount Tavern.

John's great-great-great uncle, Archibald Campbell, was a Redcoat, a colonel who, upon arrival in Boston, which had been taken over by the Rebels, honourably surrendered, but was transferred to a public jail in Concord. There is a letter from General Washington saying that he must be treated properly as a prisoner-of-war. Eventually, Archie, as we call him, was exchanged with Ethan Allen. We inherited Archie's tea pot, so both tea pots had arrived on the Isle of Canna.

Now I thought this was extremely interesting, and I told John's aunts about the exchange, and Olive said, 'Ethan Allen and *six men* were exchanged for Sir Archibald!' I thought Ethan might come in the night and bust up the china after that!

Gradually, we got water and plumbing into the farm workers' cottages and crofts. When I first arrived, the wife at the farmhouse said, 'I don't like to speak of this, Mrs Campbell, but it's a matter of a toilet.' 'Look!' I said, 'we're going to have a bathroom put in as soon as we can.' 'Oh, it isn't that. It would be just an outside . . .' 'Do you mean to say that you have *none*? No privy? And no water in the house?' 'We have a tap in the byre, but they never put water in the house.'

The dairy was filthy. The milk was set out in big pans and you took the cream off with a scooper. In order to keep the milk clean, they had pieces of canvas stretched above them . . . but they were sagging and filthy too. The dairy maid had been on Canna all her life. She was a great admirer of the Thoms; she was suspicious of all we were doing. I wasn't getting the amount of milk we should have had and almost no cream. When I went down and asked if we couldn't have more milk, she said, '*Cows are not machines*, Mrs Campbell!' Here I was, owning three cows, and unable to get milk past this fierce woman. John met someone once who said how she loved to stop at Canna when she was a young girl on her yacht, because the dairy maid would give her a glass of cream. That was where our cream was going!

I got my dander up, and I went back down the next day and said, 'Now, Mary and I (Mary was the little girl from Barra who was helping me in the house) are coming to clean the dairy tomorrow at nine o'clock. We'll be whitewashing, and I don't want anybody coming into the dairy.' I got Big Hector to mix the whitewash, and we put on sou'westers and oilskins and washed the cobwebs and dirt from the ceilings and shelves. We cleaned and scoured from top to bottom. It took us all day long. Annie would stick her head in, black as a thundercloud, and I'd say 'Go away; we're not finished yet.'

When the war was starting, John MacNeil, who had a cow named Lettie over at the Point House on the west end of Sanday, was going off to the Navy. I said, 'I'll take the cow.' So I bought Lettie and put her in the stable at the end of the bothy. The ploughman's wife, who had a new baby, milked the cow, who was harder to milk than four chair legs. Lettie didn't like me, and she wouldn't give her milk. You have to know a cow and have a feel for a cow before she'll oblige. So I would hold the baby while Kate milked, and then I'd take it up to the house and give the ploughman his milk and I had mine. And I'd make butter in a little churn. This made Annie so angry that she retired. Lettie then went down and joined the other cows. For many years after we had good fresh milk. Jesse MacKinnon and then Mary Ann MacLean were the dairy maids, skimming the cream and making butter. After they retired, there was no one to take over, so we had to sell the cows and Canna was left without a cow for the first time in a thousand years.

Canna was once part of the endowment of the famous monastery on Iona, founded by St Columba in the sixth century. After the Reformation, a thousand years later, it became part of the possessions of the Clanranald branch of the great MacDonald Clan. The Clanranalds also owned several other islands in the Hebrides and estates on the neighbouring mainland where their chief lived in Castle Tioram in Moidart. So Canna had had five owners in its long history, the Church, the Clanranald MacDonalds, until they sold it to a merchant, MacNeill from Campbeltown in 1835, who sold it again in 1882 to Robert G. Thom. It was from his grandsons that John Campbell bought it in 1938. From our first days on the island, I have felt that one never owns Canna; you serve it.

It was Angus MacDonald, the retired farm-manager (or *grieve* as he is called in the Highlands) who took me on a long walk to give me the Gaelic place names. Angus – known as '*Aonghus Eachainn*' – had great knowledge of Gaelic and when the Professor of Gaelic at Oxford came to call, he was correcting him, saying 'It's myself that should be the professor!' His son, always called 'Big Hector', was our grieve and our great friend.

There were also MacLeods and MacKinnons who had come originally from Skye, countless years before. Donald MacLeod was a gardener and lived with his sister Kate in a little cottage far up the hillside with the finest view in Canna. Donald spent years on the mainland and his speech was either Gaelic or broad Scots which took me a time to understand. We had a bond in our appreciation of cats. He shared my grief when a buzzard took an enchanting little kitten from near the kitchen door. Donald's grey hair stood straight up; he had a luxurious moustache and his shaggy eyebrows nearly concealed the bright and lively blue eyes. I would hear him in the garden having serious conversations with the Siamese tom-cat, no doubt about the holes the latter had dug in the seed beds. The cat would answer in the same tone. While Donald rested on his spade, a robin would perch on it. When the darkest day of the War came with the news of the retreat from Dunkirk, I went out to share my fear with Donald. His reply was 'WAIT YOU! They'll no beat the British!' That gave me a rising hope that stayed with me.

In those early days, our phone was inoperative after 6 p.m. On more than one occasion, the fishing boats have been very helpful. Canna has the only deep harbour in the Small Isles, so fishing boats come in at night in all seasons and of course when gales threaten. We would exchange fresh vegetables for fresh fish. One night an American visitor was taken very ill at night. The phone was not operative, so I went down to the pier and asked if they could call on their radio telephone for a doctor. They couldn't reach Mallaig for the hills, but they said, 'Don't worry. We'll find somebody.' They phoned a boat out in the Atlantic which then phoned Oban and they phoned Dr Maclean on Eigg, next door. That was 11 p.m. at night and he was here at 5 a.m. in the morning. It would have been two or three days otherwise.

When I tried to pay them, they wouldn't hear of it, so I took them down a basket of bottles of beer. They said they were very sorry: they didn't drink; they were Plymouth Brethren. But they asked for cigarettes. I think I had one packet and I gave them that; no others on the island. They are the ones who use the Presbyterian church. I can tell because the Bibles have been moved around, now and then. They conduct a little service in there. When the hand-carved collection plate was stolen, they put a call out on their radio. As they told me, 'Mrs Campbell, no fisherman would ever steal from a church!' But they hoped to shame a yachtsman into returning it. But it never came back and we now must keep its replacement in Canna House until there are regular services.

Shortly after the war, our telephone was connected to the main-land by cable and this was weak at best and sometimes cut in half by ships' anchors. We were given a radio link, a vast improvement. An important man from the London post office, along with engineers, arrived to inaugurate it. We had a splendid lunch for these guests and the Londoner sitting at my right reminded me that, for such a remote island with thirty inhabitants, we were most fortunate to have this great acquisition. I told him that two young men from this island had given their lives for this country and I thought it was the custom that the huge metropolitan areas paid for the far parts of the country to have such facilities. The tremendous sacrifice of these islands in helping to win the war made them deserving of every help the government could give.

John can look at a field and tell at once what's wrong with it by the kinds of weeds that are growing, but there was no need to instruct the grieve, the shepherds, or the other workers, because they were experienced and knew their work. He let them do what they'd been doing. The improvements were in fencing and draining, and the sheep stock had to be improved. They appreciated that he worked with them.

The first year, Martin Freeman the Irish scholar was with us on a visit. He said, 'You know Mr McCallum the cattle valuer said to me that John should not be seen running around with a butterfly net because they will laugh at him. And he should not speak Gaelic to the employees because that's not done.' But of course it was no time before they were bringing him funny bugs they didn't recognise, and they loved the fact that he spoke Gaelic to them and *wanted* to hear their stories, and that he could get old Angus MacLeod to tell him so much of what's gone into *Canna: The Story of a Hebridean Island*. It was all proved on our twenty-fifth anniversary. They gave us a party and presented us with a travelling clock and an illuminated address. We never looked back.

Mairi Anndra had taught me how to gather the oats so that when I went in the fields Big Hector was amazed that I knew how to make a stook. Also I had to skin rabbits and do all kinds of things that they didn't think the lady of the house knew how to do, but living on a croft had taught me. I once had thirteen lambs in the kitchen, brought in during a storm of high wind and cold rain. They all survived. When the shepherd would bring one, a limp little rag about to die, the first thing I did was to put it in the warming oven of my big Esse cooker while I heated milk and added a little lactic acid to keep it from making lumps in their little bellies. Then I would rub the lamb with a towel, gently stroking under the tail until it passed water – this was most important. When each lamb had had a little suck from a baby's bottle, it would come to life in a wonderful way. A big Cheviot lamb had a broken hip which was impossible to hold with a straight splint, so I used a butter-paddle (we made butter balls in those days), and this proved the thing.

Of all the lambs, the Blackface are the sturdiest, most intelligent and amusing. Two of them, the tops of their heads a mass of tight black curls, I named Vicki and Lulu. In no time they were gambolling around the kitchen table to the cats' alarm. They spent the summer with me and were special pets. The sad time came when they had to join the other sheep and lambs to go on the special ferry to Oban where they would be sold at the Mart with the great gathering of sheep from the other islands. I travelled by the passenger ferry to be there before them. Late at night, when I was in bed at the very top of the hotel, I heard the sheep coming ashore from their boat – such resounding *baas* as they were driven through the street! Was it possible that I could hear the *baas* of Vicki and Lulu above the others? The next morning I met our shepherd. 'You did hear Vicki and Lulu. They refused to be gathered with the others, ran along the pavement, standing on their hind legs to peer in the shop windows. But you will be pleased to know they have been bought along with the others by Mr Brown of Tiree to join his breeding flock. They will have a good home.'

There were pigs to be fed and I found that one had to keep them ahead when carrying the two buckets of food. They had a habit of approaching from behind and giving a butt to the knees which could tip over yourself as well as the buckets. The sows were the menace; the old boar, Charlie, was a gentleman and stayed well aside to wait his turn. They were a breed called Large White, except for a black Berkshire called 'Blanche' with an up-turned snout, pitifully ugly and a disposition to match. The only time I had to climb a wall was to avoid her as she charged down the road in a fury. She had good reason, for her piglets had been taken away, and she was ready to attack anyone in sight.

There were hill cattle, very important to the economy of the island, but among them were two or three Highlanders and they looked pretty fine to me, and I said to Donald MacLeod that I wished we had a Highland herd. He told me that Mr Thom had had a Highland herd around 1910 and they did very well here. So I sent one of the men over to the sales in South Uist to bring back some Highland heifers and he brought back three. Donald then said that there was a very good Highland bull being sold on Kerrera, and that I could get him cheap. So I bought him for £35 – elderly, but in good health, and the length of a room. I was told that I could not have found a better sire for my herd.

John was away at the time, and while the grieve found no fault, the head-shepherd was furious that I had done this without consulting either of them. When John returned, he was of the same opinion; he said they were nothing but hair, bone and hide and of no profit. But Ernest Nelson of Oban sent Colonel Reginald Fellows to inspect my small herd, and he pronounced them pure bred, assuring me that they would be entered in the herd-book. And so they were, and two years later I got a prize at the Oban sales. They always did well. John then took them over and gave the calves Gaelic names and kept their records. They proved to be a profit in time.

Within a few days of it starting, the war was brought to Canna. Two trawlers were fishing near the island when one was torpedoed.

The crew escaped in their life-boat and were rowing in a heavy sea toward another trawler when it disappeared with no one saved. A member of that crew was washed ashore here next day with his name on his oilskin coat. He was given a funeral and buried in our graveyard. With his name and the name of the trawler, I was able to write to his widow. Then we were told by HM Government that we were never to bury anyone washed ashore without a policeman and a doctor from the mainland who could prove that it was not a murder on our part! The next man was found at the far end of the island and was ten days under a tarpaulin before the weather was reasonable enough to allow a boat to cross from Mallaig with the police and doctor aboard. After this, whoever came ashore was far beyond recognition and was buried without notifying HMG. Every morning, the men would walk along the shore before we women ventured out.

We would stand on the little knoll behind the farm and watch the convoy of ships, as many as sixty, come from the Sound of Mull where they had gathered to sail north up the Minch, bound for Russia or America. If one was sunk, the others were to proceed without stopping. The submarines would be waiting and we would hear the terrific explosions, one so near that it broke the glass of my green-house. The worst thing I can remember was seeing a rocky cove on Sanday filled with little blue caps of Navy ratings. As we later learned, the *Queen Mary* – which was, of course, a troop ship – had cut right through a destroyer.

The first time a submarine was seen nearby, two men saw a periscope moving along between Canna and Skye. They rushed to the post-office to warn the Admiralty, for the post-mistress had the only phone, the kind with a handle. She wouldn't allow them to phone; only John MacLeod the coast-guard was to use it in emergencies, and he was five miles away at the far end of the island trapping rabbits and would not be home for hours. When the Admiralty did get the message, they then gave permission that we could thereafter phone at once.

The *Attendant*, a repair ship, anchored in Canna harbour for the night, on her way to the Outer Islands to attend a damaged ship. But during the night, a screaming gale from the west blew her out of the bay, and she ended with her stern on the rocks, under six-hundred-foot cliffs on the north shore of Canna. In the pitch black night, the crew were able to get into their dinghy and row away from the violent surf to wait until the first light showed them a piece of low-lying land where they could get ashore, though it was so rough that they lost their boat in saving themselves. They saw a lonely cottage and reaching the door, pounded and shouted. But the man inside refused to open. He was a shepherd and very deaf, and he was terrified as he thought they were Germans. But his little boy of seven at last understood and brought them inside. He then ran the three miles to tell us the news. John drove the little Ford truck without sides down the rough road which skirts the edge of precipices and brought all eight to the house. They told me afterwards that they were more frightened of the ride than of their time in the dinghy on the sea. They were soaked to the skin and hungry. Finding enough dry clothes was a problem, but their one worry was that they had had to leave their dog on board. However, at low tide the Canna men were able to reach The *Attendant* whose stern was high and dry and brought their big mongrel ashore to join them.

The next day, two young girls wishing to see this ship stuck on the rocks climbed the hill behind the house to the edge of the cliff. They came back to say that they hadn't seen any wreck but there was a long grey boat with a kind of house on top right in under the cliff making brown smoke. It was, of course, a German submarine recharging batteries and probably getting water from the streams descending just there. When the war ended, thirty submarines came into Kyle to surrender.

The crew was joined by an official, Mr Holden of the British Iron and Steel who owned the ship, so there were nine men to take care of for a week. We were fortunate in having hens and cows so eggs, milk, and butter were plentiful. I had laid in a store of tinned ham and fruit, sugar and tea, when it was still possible to buy these things; now they were rapidly devoured. When Mr Holden asked me what his company owed me, I said nothing – but I would appreciate if they could replace the tea and sugar which were severely rationed. Even the British Iron and Steel could not do that, but they did send me a cheque for twenty-five pounds. All the crew were from Ulster, County Down, and nicer more appreciative men one could not meet. The Captain McBurney and the other members not only wrote to me, but sent presents, including a damask tablecloth.

All the while, we had two huge tea boxes containing tea, sugar and biscuits which we were to open only if invaded! Near the end of the war, a government official arrived to examine the boxes. He prised open the lids and then, seated at the kitchen table, he counted every item. All were there. He then nailed back the lids and had the boxes sent south.

Throughout the war, the only flour we could get was a compound of wheat and chalk with, we were told, 'nutriments added'. An archaeologist guest described the scene where the chalk was taken, somewhere near Cambridge on a hillside of an ancient cemetery. One morning the shore was strewn with huge sacks of Canadian flour. The salt water had made a casing that preserved the contents. A sharp knife split the bag to reveal flour from Heaven, white and pure. I had yeast from a Glasgow baker and made bread, rolls, cinnamon buns, the like of which we have never had before nor since.

Travelling became difficult when we could not leave the island without a permit, for which we had to write to the Army Office in Edinburgh. This would take three weeks, so we had to plan well ahead of time for any journey. On one occasion my permit had not arrived in time for me to travel with the head shepherd and the bullocks to be sold at Dingwall, a town close to Inverness on the east coast, but the friendly policeman in our port of Mallaig told me not to worry. I could take the boat that called here on her way to the Outer Islands, which would eventually round north of Skye, then reaching Kyle of Lochalsh where I would take the train to Dingwall. He would explain to the policeman there who I was and there would be no trouble.

When I reached Kyle of Lochalsh I was met by a suspicious policeman who put me straight away in the dingy little waiting-room of the station and told me not to leave the room until the train left. Sitting on the hard bench were two elderly and bewildered ladies with a little dog on a string. Their sad story was that they had taken the train at Dingwall for Auchnasheen to have tea with a friend, and when they came to their station the little dog had got caught under the seat and they were carried on to Kyle. It was then 2.30 and the train left after 5 p.m. We consoled each other and the sad little dog. Then the door flew open – the stationmaster saying, 'Quick, quick! The policeman's away for his tea. Hurry up the road a bit to yon wee hut and you'll get a cup yourselves.' We hurried and had a cup which restored us, then back to be seated on the bench when the policeman returned to see us aboard the train.

I noticed as we left the station a flat-topped freight car with large grey round balls, barely concealed under a yellow tarpaulin – mines! When I reached Dingwall, on the east coast, I found our cattleman there before me with the bullocks to be sold at the Mart. No permit necessary for that area, nor nearby Inverness, all open to the North Sea with the Germans in Norway! (We had heard exciting stories of the brave Norwegians escaping in anything from fishing boats to dinghies, landing on the safe shore of Scotland, from Leith to the Shetlands.)

I went into Mrs Soutar's small shop where there were patterns, wools, and newspapers for sale. The summer before, I had bought two volumes of flute solos by the eighteenth-century composer James Hook, so she knew I was interested in music. She brought out from the back of the shop two orange boxes filled with treasures: Beethoven quartets, Schubert trios, the complete set of Schumann songs, Mendelssohn piano pieces and so much else. The chamber music was published by Breitkopf and Hartel, which I knew was of great value as that publishing house had been destroyed. I told her that I could not afford to buy what she offered, that it was priceless. She then told me that it had come from Brahan Castle near by, the home of the late Countess of Seaforth, and that she was a German and a musician. Mrs Soutar was certain that she would never find anyone else who would appreciate the music; she had known the Countess and felt sure that she would be pleased to have me take it. For £10 I brought home these treasures which have been a joy beyond words to this house.

We've never allowed shooting on Canna; it's a sort of sanctuary for man, beast and bird, so to speak. Nobody is to use a gun. One day during the war, I was painting the little back bedroom when I heard a gun go off – two or three rifle shots. So I ran as fast as I could to the pier and as I ran I saw the eider ducks which always come on the skerry near the pier to sun themselves. There were three fishing boats tied up and I called, 'Who has the gun? It's absolutely forbidden to shoot the duck and I will report it to the police!' And I said some other things. I had been followed by a guest in the house, a Catholic schoolteacher from Yorkshire, very proper. She came running after me: 'Margaret! I didn't know you had such words as you said to them!' 'You haven't heard anything! I'll damn them all to hell without any trouble.'

I went back to the house and got John and we went out in the boat and lifted eleven dead eiders that had just been sitting in the sun, a sure shot. I then telephoned the police and they said, 'Which boat?' And I told them, 'I think it was such and such, but I'm not absolutely certain. But I do know that anybody with a gun shooting in the bay – *that* is forbidden because of the ricochet.' I didn't say anything more, but I was going off to Mallaig in the morning and I stopped in at the police station.

'Well, do you have evidence?'

'Yes. We have the ducks we took up. We've buried them in the garden, but we can dig them up for you.'

He was a pale-faced, miserable looking thing and he said to me: 'Mrs Campbell, you see they might do something to you in return. You see, they might do some damage on Canna if you pursue this.'

'Well,' I said, 'I see what I should do is to go to Skye and consult a witch!'

Whereupon his eyes opened and his jaw fell; he was absolutely shaken with this. Now the interesting thing is that Skye had always had a reputation for witches, all through history. I have a suspicion that the policeman was a Skyeman! Anyway, needless to say, he did nothing about it, but his superior was looking out for them and they caught a man who was shooting deer on Rum. He was the man who killed the eiders. He had no licence and that fixed it. They never bothered about ducks on Canna, but shooting deer was much more serious, especially with meat rationing.

During the war, huge square kites of thin canvas were tied to the stern of a ship with long wires which were supposed to entangle a dive bomber. Of course they often broke loose and one day we had one come ashore on Canna. We contacted the Admiralty and they were going to come and collect it. That was in the summer but they never came. The next summer John made a little sail for the dinghy and he sailed all over the bay. Meanwhile the thing had just gone into sticks; he'd brought it back and wrapped it up. One day I looked out and here was an armed trawler, and eleven men were coming up the road to collect the kite that had been reported over a year before. I saw John going by the window and I wanted to reach him before they did so I brought them into the living room/drawing room. I signalled to John who went around to the morning room and gathered up the remains and tied it with string. And this rubbish was handed to them.

These men on the armed trawlers were big, able-bodied men. The islanders were furious with them because while their men were in the gravest danger, captured at El Alamein and elsewhere, *they* were just coasting around here. They'd been taken out of prison, the worst riff-raff. One night I was by myself in the house. It was late autumn, pitch black. About one o'clock in the morning I heard pounding on the door. Fortunately I hadn't gone to bed, so I came down with a candle and here were two men, one with a very bad gash over his eye, bleeding. The other man said angrily, 'I had to knock all this time.' I didn't dare let on there was no one else in the house, so I said, 'Now don't wake everybody. Come in.' And I sat them down. The one with the cut looked as if he might faint and I said to him, 'Put your head down between your knees and I'll get the stuff to tidy you up.' The mean one said, 'He'll need a whisky or a brandy.' 'I've got very little brandy and it's only for medicinal purposes. I'll give your friend a little tot.'

I'd been taught that if there's a bad cut and you cannot stitch it, you fold over a piece of adhesive tape double and then cut triangles, but not quite into the centre. One piece of adhesive on one side and another across from it and that little bit in the middle pulls it together, almost as good as a stitch. A butterfly bandage. The poor man was so miserable and had such a sore head that he could only be pleasant and thank me. The other one was something else.

John had to be away for long intervals and I was left in charge of the island. Everyone was understanding and helpful with one exception, the head-shepherd, who could not accept a woman in her husband's place. To add to his irritation, he was not on friendly terms with Murdo, the shepherd, who had the Blackface flock at the west end of the island. Their quarrelling ended in a serious fight when Murdo attacked him with a bushman's saw and they rolled together down a long grassy slope. The only wound was a nick on the bridge of the head shepherd's nose. When Murdo came to see me after the fray, he admitted that he had a fierce temper, hard to control, and I sympathised with his just anger. He said that he must leave, which

I understood, but there was the problem of the government not allowing a farm servant to leave in war without serious cause.

I phoned the Labour Office and gave an irate man the details. I was told that that was no reason and that he would deal with this man with a saw. While he was giving me a tirade, I put down the receiver and told Murdo he was free to go. He had found a place for a shepherd on the mainland across from the Isle of Mull. Since I had to report at Oban, which was on his way to his new job, we travelled together with his wife, child, a box of cats, a cow and many belongings. We sailed from Canna to Lochboisdale, South Uist, where we changed to another boat to go south. In the early morning, we called at Tiree and Coll, and then we all joined to have a picnic breakfast on deck. I waved them ashore at Kilchoan on the mainland near his future home while I continued to Oban.

I had to report there to the authorities that I was exempt from being called up to His Majesty's Service. As the war extended, all women under forty-eight were called to work at anything from munitions to agriculture. It was being a farmer's wife which got me off, but it riled me to be put through a third degree of questioning by a young woman who kept knitting while she voiced her suspicions, raised by my American voice and the fact that my husband was a laird. But I was allowed to return to Canna by the same long journey.

Canna's safe harbour, known since Viking times, has brought yachts from all the airts, not only Scotland but France, Holland, Ireland and the USA. Many have returned year after year with skippers and crew who have become our dear friends. One tiny yacht – she could not have been forty feet in length and without an engine – sailed from Rhode Island, skippered by Professor John Coolidge of Columbia University. He was only a mile off his bearings when he reached the shore of Ireland. The yachts are the summer visitors, but fishing boats from the port of Mallaig or the east coast of Scotland come into Canna harbour all year round. On a winter's night, several tied alongside the pier and others moored in the bay give a vision of a town with their many lights. In summer they spread their nets on the fields nearby to clean and mend them. They are friends to us all and generous in giving fish which are so appreciated, even by the cats.

Kathleen Raine described it well in her book *The Oval Portrait and Other Poems*:

Canna House, 1975
For John and Margaret

The cards that brighten the New Year,
A Christmas-tree grown in the wood,
The crimson curtains drawn, the owl
Whose porcelain holds a lamp to read
The music on the Steinway grand
Piano with its slipping scores
Of Couperin, Chopin and Ravel –
John and Margaret Campbell made
This room to house the things they treasure,
Records of Scotland's speech and song,
Lore of butterfly and bird,
And velvet cats step soft among
Learned journals on the floor.

Since our first years on Canna, through the war until now, Canna has been a refuge, a restorer to many. Poets and painters, archaeologists and naturalists, musicians and scholars – all have found inspiration and pleasure in the life and beauty of Canna. Compton Mackenzie was one of our first guests, he being most interested in John's plan of bringing Canna to a first-rate farm. His wife Faith came, writing her novel *The Crooked Wall*, and playing the piano magnificently. She had studied with a pupil of Clara Schumann's and the 'Carnaval' and 'Papillon' were the source. The fun of playing duets – old warhorses like the overtures to 'Coriolanus', 'Egmont', and 'Figaro', John adding to the bass with the French horn.

Vivien Mackie, a professional cellist and star pupil of Casals, would come with her precious ancient instrument (glorious tone!) in a case that could serve as a bank vault. It was interesting to see the cats come in to enjoy Bach, but when Bartók began they would file out with tails standing straight.

Distinguished artists have stayed with us through the years: Roland Svensson of Sweden, Gilbert Spencer, Helen Binyon, Winifred Nicolson and Reynolds Stone. And there have been two well-known poets on Canna, the Scottish Helen Cruickshank and the English Kathleen Raine. I first met Helen on the road-side in Barra. Annie Johnston, the folklorist, and an elderly friend and I were on our way to a picnic on the shore and we asked her to join us. While we were eating our sandwiches in a wet mist, I recited a poem I had found in *Punch* long before in New York which I loved enough to memorize:

> I met a man in Harris tweed
> As I went down the strand.
> I turned and followed like a dog
> The breath of hill and sea and bog
> That hung about the crotal brown.

'I wrote that,' she said, amazed that I should have it, but that was nothing to my delight in meeting her. From that day, we became friends, and her house at Corstorphine was a refuge to me as it has been to a vast number of others.

Canna is so rich in flora and fauna that ornithologists, entomologists, geologists and archaeologists, both professionals and the eager amateurs, have been constant guests. The latter remind me of a poem I was taught as a child about Robinson Crusoe taking his domestic animals on such excursions:

And we gather as we travel
Bits of moss and dirty gravel,
And we chip off little specimens of stone,
And we carry home as prizes
Funny bugs of handy sizes
Just to give the day a scientific tone.

Among our guests was an entomologist, an authority on moths. John's acquaintance with him had been through letters. He was objectionable on arrival, and though I had long been accustomed to eccentrics, he was beyond that. He found John's collections of absorbing interest, but with me his manners were appalling. After a scene with me, John came to the kitchen to tell me that this was a sign of exhibitionism, and I would know all about it if I read Havelock Ellis. I said I had no need to read Havelock Ellis and when was he going to leave? But that day arrived our good friend Gavin Maxwell, and when our guest found Gavin, another Etonian, he was filled with supreme joy. (As an American, I thought this only applied to Masons.) His manners at once moderated and a reminiscing bore was an easier affliction until his departure.

There have been many distinguished scientists among our visitors: Peter Wormell and Dr Morton Boyd of the Nature Conservancy with their vast knowledge of all the fields of nature. Bristowe, collecting his spiders; E.B. Ford, Teddy Pelham-Clinton, Geoffrey Harper and his son Michael, George Waterston, Robert Swann and John Love who re-introduced the sea eagle on Rum from Norway, seen regularly now on Canna. We have never allowed the Viking graves to be dug or the site of a Columban nunnery to be disturbed, but our friend T.E. Lethbridge excavated some small sites of very early dwellings. There have been other archaeologists who took photographs and made drawings of the carved stones and crosses.

Among the few discordants that have come ashore was a Canadian lady who had sent a wire to announce her arrival, thinking we had a private hotel. Handsome, well dressed – I much envied her jodhpurs – and inclined to peremptory judgements, she was delighted to find she was visiting a private house. Such love she had for all God's creatures and welcomed Pooni, our big Siamese, on her lap. He was my pride – deep blue eyes, a knot at the tip of his tail and his light fawn coat thick and soft. It was his character that made us love him – intelligent, affectionate, loyal. She said that I seemed to have many cats; I replied that I bred Siamese and got good prices for the kittens. 'I would think,' she said, as she ran her hands through his coat, 'that you could get far more money for the pelts.' I could not think of any words but that I would nail her own hide to the barn door before I would skin a cat, so I left the room.

All my life I have had cats as companions. In Glenshaw we had fine toms with Old Testament names. Tiglath-Pilezar was a favourite of mine. At the Studio Club, a huge eunuch – black and white – would ascend the fire escape to spend evenings with me. He belonged to elderly Germans who had a shop of elegant baby clothes below. In South Uist, I found that Mairi Anndra had the same love of cats, and when I married she gave me Wicked Willy who accompanied me to Canna where his fourth-generation descendant is with me today. All have been exactly like their forebear, woolly brown tabbies with magnificent tails.

The Island of Canna is a paradise for cats, no traffic nor traps, a world of their own to explore, fields and woods, moor and high hills, good hunting for rabbits and always a fireside with plentiful food as well as being petted and enjoyed. The continuous tribe through the years of Siamese and domestic cats included one Abyssinian warrior. He was the tallest, the heaviest and the boss, and his name was Leo. There was also a half-Siamese I called Reuben, a large tabby with saffron chest. He was timid but not with me. We had a bond and when I was busy cooking at the stove he would sit on the table beside me while I sang 'Reuben, Reuben, I've been thinking/what a sad world it would be/if all the cats would be transported/far across the western sea'. He disappeared to my sorrow and for three years was never seen. I was told by a priest that I had given him the wrong name. The Reuben in the Bible was as 'unstable as water'.

Three years later my sister Martha died. She was the one of all my family and relations who was interested in my life in the Hebrides and proud of my little achievements. I was worse than bereft when I heard the news and that dreary December night I said aloud in my misery – 'Oh Martha, give me a sign.' Early in the morning John turned on the light in the living-room to find Reuben sitting on the floor as though he had never left home. He was looking his best, amazingly tame. After making a fuss of me, he then jumped in the hot-cupboard which had been his favourite bed so long ago. He stayed with us for six months and then vanished, never to be seen again.

There have never been deer or foxes on the island nor, to my relief, adders. Rabbits are more than plentiful, and they were our main dish during the war years. I learnt to skin and serve them in a variety of ways. I found that letting them soak in salt water took away the rabbit taste and guests who said they couldn't eat them were deceived into thinking they were chicken. The brown Norwegian rat was a problem, for they had taken up residence in the house when it was empty and refused to take us seriously until we increased our number of cats. Mice rarely come in the house, and if we see one, it is to be protected, it is such a charming creature, with large brown eyes and cream colour underneath. It is a Hebridean type of wood-mouse. There are tiny shrews that the cats sometimes catch but never eat for they have a horrid taste. They are very pugnacious and one can hear their quarrelling squeaks in the long grass in the garden. We introduced hedgehogs to defeat the mammoth slugs that infested the vegetable garden. But they found the woods more comfortable when they multiplied, and only visit us now and then. Otters live along the shore; they are not often seen, but they have special places where a small stream comes to a sandy cove between the rocks. There they have their place to play and the sand is covered with their little footprints and the swathe from their tails.

At the far west end of Canna is where the Atlantic or great grey seal breeds. It is in autumn when the pups are born. I remember one Christmas Eve on Canna when we heard a strange call we thought might be wild duck. When we opened the front door we heard a voice like a child. We went down to our jetty with a torch and there was a baby seal whose eyes were like gold coins. It had been left there by the mother while she swam in the bay, and then returning to collect it when the tide came in. A Christmas greeting!

When you live on an island, strange things wash ashore. One day there was a large motor-boat in the harbour, and soon a woman appeared at the door in oilskins and enormous pearl earrings, a sou'wester and a basket.

'Mrs Campbell?'

'Yes?'

'Would you bake me some scones?'

'Bake you some scones? What's the matter; haven't you any bread?'

'Well, we do have some bread, but we like to have something to munch on deck, my boys.'

'I only bake for fishermen who are stranded here without bread.'

'Well, I wonder if you have any vegetables?'

'Yes, what do you want?'

'Potatoes . . . and green vegetables.'

And I said, 'If you go down to the road and walk along to the left, you'll see the potato field. There's a fork at the end of the furrow, and you can dig yourself some potatoes. And when you come back, I'll show you where the vegetables are.' She came back with two potatoes. Obviously, she didn't know how or where to dig. So I took her up to Tighard and showed her the garden. She arrived back down, and she had peas and lettuce and various things in her basket, and she said, 'How much do I owe you?'

'Well,' I said, 'you don't owe me anything, but what we ask is that you give something to the Sacred Heart Hospital at Daliburgh in South Uist which is in great need of money. Here's the jar.'

'Well, I don't know what to put in.'

'Well,' I said, 'what do you pay for your vegetables?'

'Oh, I never buy my vegetables.' She gave me half a crown for all this. And that was that, though soon after, some Eriskay fishermen came to pick gooseberries and left a ten-shilling note in the jar.

The next year, while I was washing the kitchen floor one day, this apparition appeared at the back door, a man with her in a smart yachting costume. 'Mrs Campbell! Do you remember me?'

'I'll never forget you; what would you like?'

'We'd like some of your lovely vegetables.'

'You know where to find them' – this time she had two baskets – 'and the jar is on the front steps. You can put the money in the jar.' And she put in another half crown for two baskets of vegetables.

Another visitor arrived from the British Council. Her job was to carry out a census of households in the Highlands and Islands to determine how many used their ovens. 'Well,' I said, 'if you asked me that, I'd say it was none of your business. Why in the world are you asking them about their ovens?' Said she: 'They boil everything on top and that's why they all have bad teeth. All the goodness goes out of the meat.' I replied that the best teeth in the world were on the Isle of Lewis where they boil everything on the stove and that most of the thatched houses didn't have ovens at all. 'This is crazy!' I told her. 'And don't you go about asking anybody here, because it's offensive.'

Many visitors have regarded us as very second-class and think we ought to be only too pleased and anxious to help them, to entertain them. Once I was typing up in my sitting room on a lovely summer day (this was in the sixties) and I suddenly heard voices. The front door was standing wide open. I got up to see who it might be and walked to the head of the stairs, and there were two men standing on the stairs studying the big map of Canna. I said, 'What do you want?' 'Eggs.' 'Eggs? How did you get in?' 'The door was open. There didn't seem to be anyone about.' Very Oxford-Cambridge. I said, 'You *never* walk into a private house!' And they went right on ahead of me out the front door without saying another word.

So I told Brucie Watt, the Captain of the *Western Isles*, a boat chartered for cruises out of Mallaig, and Brucie said, 'You must have a dog.' Time passed, but one day I was coming back on Brucie's boat and he said to me: 'I have a parcel for you.' I thought it was very strange that he went down into the hold with me to a passenger compartment. He had a cardboard box there which he opened and there was this tiniest puppy, just about the size of my fist, this wee, wee thing – and that was Perita. Brucie had her sister. They were bred by a shepherd near Loch Hourn – a mixture of Cairn and something. They had Cairn heads and coats and they were very smart, with a loud bark. Brucie's 'Cheekie' would go down the hold and bring up his cigarettes.

After Perita died, I had a guardian bulldog in the form of Mr Ironsides. He had been a Glasgow bus driver and he knew how to handle people. He'd watch to see anyone going down the road to see if they were going in the gate, if they looked as if they were going to nose or pry. He'd follow them in, stalk them and then, when they came to peer in the window, he would let fly.

Canna has been inhabited since prehistoric times. I found a comrade in my interest in Canna's antiquities when Donald John MacKinnon, aged nine, asked if he could come to see me. He wanted to know about the Stone Age and guns. (He knew that I had a collection of old pistols.) With the help of *Larousse Encyclopaedia of Ancient and Medieval History* we found information about life in the Stone Age, and when we reached the Neolithic, it was

Donald John who saw the similarity between the photograph of that spiral culture and a stone that I had retrieved from a stone wall – incised with circles with a line drawn through them. His sister, Anne-Marie, brought me a shard found beside a mound excavated by rabbits. This had a pattern of chevrons and dots which Stuart Piggott, Abercrombie Professor of Prehistoric Archaeology in the University of Edinburgh, identified as the upper part of a beaker, of c.1900–1500 BC.

There are two souterraines – also referred to as 'underground dwellings' – on Canna. They are found in other parts of Scotland. Their use is debatable, but it is said that they were used to store food, and yet one in South Uist was inhabited by men in the eighteenth century. We have found shards on prehistoric sites; again, it is difficult to give any date, for the same sort of pottery was made in Lewis in the eighteenth century. Before the tenth century, Irish missionary monks were here and there are the ruined walls of a nunnery on a near-inaccessible promontory below the cliffs on the south side of the island. The name is *Sgor nam Ban Naomh*, the 'point of the holy women'.

The scourge of the Hebrides were the Norsemen who began their raids of pillage and slaughter in the eighth century. They eventually ruled the Hebrides for four centuries. Canna was a part of their domain, as the place names prove. During the war, our great friend Alf Sommerfelt, a minister of education who had escaped with King Haakon to England, visited Canna where he identified the Norse graves. There are nine mounds in a row, lying above the shore on the north side facing the Minch, pointing toward home, as he said. He thought from its size that the centre one might be a boat burial. We all agreed that these graves should never be disturbed. So many others have been opened, and they all reveal the same artefacts. It would be right to leave these graves in peace.

There is a Viking grave at Langanes, rifled very many years ago. Only an outline of stones remains. It is down on the grassy slope by the sea, and the tradition is that anyone disturbing it again will bring on fierce storms. An important archeologist from Edinburgh called it a shieling and said he never took tradition seriously. Now, shielings were shelters or little huts built far up on hillsides, usually composed of sod with a stone end for a fireplace. It is where women go with the cows in summer to keep them away from the hay and oat fields. There they would make butter and cheese, storing it until the harvest was over when they would bring the cows down to graze again on the stubble. The shieling I visited on Lewis had one end filled with fresh heather for a wide bed. The Viking grave was far too narrow for two people to sleep, and besides, it would not be a place for a shieling. But I suppose it will now be published in the archaeological accounts as a shieling.

At the east end of Canna was a village called Keill. It was cleared of people in 1849; the stones of their houses make the beautiful walls which surround the fields. In the centre, there had been a church dating from Viking times or before; it was completely erased and the graveyard ploughed. A new graveyard was made a short distance away and the old gravestones were taken there, many carved with Celtic designs. The grieve at that time hated any elaborate carving associated with Roman Catholicism, so he had these stones broken; they were said to have been used in building the second storey of his house. But there were three stones which the men could not bear to break, so they buried them and never told where. And one family descended from the chief of Clanranald saved his stone to put on their family grave in the new graveyard, a fine incised slab of micaceous schist, with a figure of a warrior with a sword, along with other symbols.

The Thoms had kept a stele, broken in half. It was found in a wall and had been reported with a drawing in J. Romilly Allen's *Early Christian Monuments of Scotland* (1903). On one side is part of a man in a short tunic with a serpent wound around his legs. On the obverse are two different decorations: a block of what is known as key pattern, and an elaborate design of four garfish, their tails intertwined and their heads in the four corners. In my search for any broken fragments of stone in the wall around the new graveyard, I saw the top of a stone near-buried and away from any grave. In putting my fingers down through the soil, I felt carving. To my enormous delight, I found on dragging it out that it was a third piece of the stele – the man's belt and his arms crossed on his breast. I have still to find his head.

All that remains in the field now called 'Keill' is a standing Celtic cross of the ninth century, eight feet high. It is missing all but one of its arms; there is a tradition that they were shot off in target practice by the press gangs during the time of the Napoleonic Wars. The same type is found in Iona; the Canna cross and those like it in Argyllshire were probably made by the Irish craftsmen travelling in the west of Scotland. Some of the carvings on the Canna cross are unique, although you find certain of the designs on Pictish stones. The dog – or what seems to be a dog – biting his back is one; the man on horseback is another. There is a strange beast at the bottom and what seems to be one of the Magi handing something to the Virgin; or that's how I see it, judging by early drawings and from what I could tell from my own photographs. On the remaining arm is a camel.

I was determined to find the floor of the church because my idea was that we would rebuild it or mark where it had been with stones. So I went over to the field with a steel curtain rod and I sounded near where the cross stands, since undoubtedly that is where the church stood. I sounded all around and got no reply and then suddenly I heard the hollow sound of stone. I dug up the brown earth and the weeds on top and moved that aside and then I came to a long, narrow flagstone which I was sure was the floor. I lifted it and the soil underneath was pitch black, quite different from the brown soil on top, and in it I found a little white stone that looked almost like an eye, the whole eyeball. I put it in my pocket and scraped away and found human bones. So I covered up everything and put back the sods so that nobody would disturb it and came back to tell what I had found.

Now grass here grows very quickly, so when I went back with John and Frank Collinson in a few days to where I thought the flagstone was, I couldn't find it. We hunted everywhere through that field and we never found it again. They said, 'Are you sure?' And I had the little white stone to prove it. We found two hearthstones that had been covered over, but we never again found the chapel floor. I think we weren't supposed to.

In 1963, in this same field of Keill, we celebrated the fourteen hundredth anniversary of St Columba's coming to Scotland. (Columba is known as *Colum Cille* – the dove of the Church; *cille* is the same word as 'Kells' and 'Keill'.) Late tradition is that Columba was here; Canna belonged to Columba's territory, so to speak – to Iona's domain. The Bishop of Argyll at that time was not interested in Columba, and when Iona offered the cathedral there for a celebration, the Bishop said no, that people should go to St Margaret's. Queen Margaret of Scotland is a saint, and she has a shrine at Dunfermline – and that's where the people should go, the Bishop said. When I heard about this from Fr Malcolm Maclellan, I said to him, 'Let's have it here!'

I let it be known that on ninth of June, St Columba's Day, there would be a gathering on Canna. Three boats came: one from Rum, one from Eigg and one from Mallaig – filled with people. We first had the Mass over in the church on Sanday, and then in the afternoon we had the Benediction in Keill. Father Donald Macdougall, a Barra man – tall and thin, beautiful in his gold vestments, with a sconser and the Host, led the procession back to Canna and up into the field where we had Jessie's kitchen table with a white cloth, candlesticks and flowers. It was the most beautiful day imaginable. It had been a slow spring, so that the grass was just green velvet, filled with buttercups and daisies ... skylarks singing and the blue sea. There was a slight breeze and in order to keep the candles from blowing out, my guest the piano tuner and our Basque friend, Saturnino Sagarzazu, and the other boys stood holding out their jackets, exactly like shags on a rock.

We counted about eighty-five people. We sang hymns – the St Columba Hymn and one in Latin. As we left, I said to Mrs Stirling, 'You know, monks were massacred in this field right about here.' And she said, 'We felt something come right out of the ground.' It was the most moving experience for everybody there. When we came back to Canna House, where we entertained everybody, I found a large dog stretched out under the piano and the house filled with people I'd never seen before. Afterwards, when I'd go to Mallaig, people on the boat I didn't know would say to me, 'I was on Canna for St Columba's Day and I will never, never forget it.'

From the Missal for St Columba's Day, here is what we heard read in the field of Keill:

> Sing the Lord a new song;
> Let His praise sound from end
> to end of the earth. Praise
> Him from the sea, all men that sail on it,
> and all creatures the sea contains;
> the islands and the island-dwellers.
> Let the wilderness, now, lift up its head,
> and the desert cities,
> the men of Cedar shall have villages to dwell in.
> Give praise then, inhabitants of Petra;
> the mountain-tops shall ring with their cries.
> All shall give God His praise,
> till the renown of Him
> reaches the islands far away.